Pressing Issues of Inequality and American Indian Communities

Pressing Issues of Inequality and American Indian Communities has been co-published simultaneously as *Journal of Poverty,* Volume 2, Number 4 1998.

The *Journal of Poverty* Monographs/"Separates"

Income Security and Public Assistance for Women and Children, edited by Keith M. Kilty, Virginia E. Richardson, and Elizabeth A. Segal

Pressing Issues of Inequality and American Indian Communities, edited by Elizabeth A. Segal and Keith M. Kilty

These books were published simultaneously as special thematic issues of the *Journal of Poverty* and are available bound separately. Visit Haworth's website at http://www.haworthpressinc.com to search our online catalog for complete tables of contents and ordering information for these and other pubications. Or call 1-800-HAWORTH (outside US/Canada: 607-722-5857), Fax: 1-800-895-0582 (outside US/Canada: 607-771-0012), or e-mail getinfo@haworthpressinc.com

Pressing Issues
of Inequality
and American Indian
Communities

Elizabeth A. Segal
Keith M. Kilty
Editors

Pressing Issues of Inequality and American Indian Communities
has been co-published simultaneously as *Journal of Poverty,* Volume 2, Number 4 1998.

The Haworth Press, Inc.
New York • London

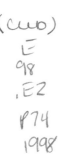

Pressing Issues of Inequality and American Indian Communities
has been co-published simultaneously as *Journal of Poverty*™,
Volume 2, Number 4 1998.

Cover design by Thomas J. Mayshock Jr.

Library of Congress Cataloging-in-Publication Data

Pressing issues of inequality and American Indian Communities / Elizabeth A. Segal, Keith M. Kilty, editors.
    p. cm.
    "Has been co-published simultaneously as Journal of poverty, Volume 2, Number 4, 1998."
    Includes bibliographical references and index.
    ISBN 0-7890-0663-4 (alk. paper)
    1. Indians of North America–Economic conditions. 2. Indians of North America–Social conditions. I. Segal, Elizabeth A. II. Kilty, Keith M. (Keith Michael), 1946- . III. Journal of poverty.
E98.E2P74 1998
305.897–dc21
                                                          98-38650
                                                            CIP

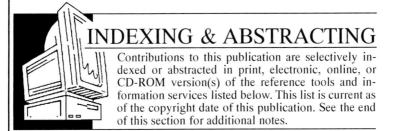

INDEXING & ABSTRACTING

Contributions to this publication are selectively indexed or abstracted in print, electronic, online, or CD-ROM version(s) of the reference tools and information services listed below. This list is current as of the copyright date of this publication. See the end of this section for additional notes.

- *Abstracts in Social Gerontology: Current Literature on Aging,* National Council on the Aging, Library, 409 Third Street SW, 2nd Floor, Washington, DC 20024

- *Abstracts of Research in Pastoral Care & Counseling,* Loyola College, 7135 Minstrel Way, Suite 101, Columbia, MD 21045

- *Alzheimer's Disease Education & Referral Center (ADEAR),* Combined Health Information Database (CHID), P.O. Box 8250, Silver Spring, MD 20907-8250

- *Applied Social Sciences Index & Abstracts (ASSIA) (Online: ASSI via Data-Star) (CDRom: ASSIA Plus),* Bowker-Saur Limited, Maypole House, Maypole Road, East Grinstead, West Sussex RH19 1HH, England

- *caredata CD: the social and community care database,* National Institute for Social Work, 5 Tavistock Place, London WC1H 9SS, England

- *Central Library & Documentation Bureau,* International Labour Office, CH-1211 Geneva 22, Switzerland

- *CNPIEC Reference Guide: Chinese National Directory of Foreign Periodicals,* P.O. Box 88, Beijing, People's Republic of China

- *Criminal Justice Abstracts,* Willow Tree Press, 15 Washington Street, 4th Floor, Newark, NJ 07102

- *Family Studies Database (online and CD/ROM),* National Information Services Corporation, 306 East Baltimore Pike, 2nd Floor, Media, PA 19063

- *FRANCIS,* INIST-CNRS, 2, allee du Parc de Brabois, F-54514 Vandoeuvre-les-Nancy, Cedex, France

(continued)

- *Health Management Information Service (HELMIS),* Nuffield Institute for Health, 71-75 Clarendon Road, Leeds LS2 9PL, England

- *Index to Periodical Articles Related to Law,* University of Texas, 727 East 26th Street, Austin, TX 78705

- *INTERNET ACCESS (& additional networks) Bulletin Board for Libraries ("BUBL") coverage of information resources on INTERNET, JANET, and other networks.*
  - <URL:http://bubl.ac.uk/>
  - The new locations will be found under <URL:http://bubl.ac.uk/link/>.
  - Any existing BUBL users who have problems finding information on the new service should contact the BUBL help line by sending e-mail to <bubl@bubl.ac.uk>.
  The Andersonian Library, Curran Building, 101 St. James Road, Glasgow G4 0NS, Scotland

- *Mental Health Abstracts (online through DIALOG),* IFI/Plenum Data Company, 3202 Kirkwood Highway, Wilmington, DE 19808

- *National Library Database on Homelessness,* National Coalition for the Homeless, 1612 K Street, NW, #1004, Homelessness Information Exchange, Washington, DC 20006

- *National Periodical Library,* Guide to Social Science and Religion, P. O. Box 3278, Clearwater, FL 33767

- *Political Science Abstracts,* IFI/Plenum Data Company, 3202 Kirkwood Highway, Wilmington, DE 19808

- *Public Affairs Information Bulletin (PAIS),* Public Affairs Information Service, Inc., 521 West 43rd Street, New York, NY 10036-4396

- *Referativnyi Zhurnal* (Abstracts Journal of the All-Russian Institute of Scientific and Technical Information), 20 Usievich Street, Moscow 125219, Russia

- *Social Work Abstracts,* National Association of Social Workers, 750 First Street NW, 8th Floor, Washington, DC 20002

- *Sociological Abstracts (SA),* Sociological Abstracts, Inc., P.O. Box 22206, San Diego, CA 92192-0206

(continued)

SPECIAL BIBLIOGRAPHIC NOTES

related to special journal issues (separates)
and indexing/abstracting

☐ indexing/abstracting services in this list will also cover material in any "separate" that is co-published simultaneously with Haworth's special thematic journal issue or DocuSerial. Indexing/abstracting usually covers material at the article/chapter level.

☐ monographic co-editions are intended for either non-subscribers or libraries which intend to purchase a second copy for their circulating collections.

☐ monographic co-editions are reported to all jobbers/wholesalers/approval plans. The source journal is listed as the "series" to assist the prevention of duplicate purchasing in the same manner utilized for books-in-series.

☐ to facilitate user/access services all indexing/abstracting services are encouraged to utilize the co-indexing entry note indicated at the bottom of the first page of each article/chapter/contribution.

☐ this is intended to assist a library user of any reference tool (whether print, electronic, online, or CD-ROM) to locate the monographic version if the library has purchased this version but not a subscription to the source journal.

☐ individual articles/chapters in any Haworth publication are also available through the Haworth Document Delivery Service (HDDS).

Pressing Issues of Inequality and American Indian Communities

CONTENTS

ABOUT THE EDITORS

Elizabeth A. Segal, PhD, MSW, is Professor in the School of Social Work at Arizona State University in Tempe. She has made many presentations and conducted workshops and seminars on various issues concerning social work, and she is the author of many articles, book chapters, book reviews, proceedings, and reports. She served as a policy analyst in Washington, DC, as an American Association for the Advancement of Science Fellow. Dr. Segal is a member of the National Association of Social Workers, the Council on Social Work Education, and the Bertha Capen Reynolds Society.

Keith M. Kilty, PhD, is Professor in the College of Social Work at Ohio State University in Columbus. He has published or presented more than 50 papers and is an editorial reviewer for *ALCOHOLISM: Clinical and Experimental Research,* the *Journal of Studies on Alcohol,* and the *American Education Research Journal,* and Assistant Editor for the *Journal of Drug Issues.* Dr. Kilty is a member of the Society for the Study of Social Problems and a member of its Committee on Standards and Freedom of Research, Publication, and Teaching, and a member and Treasurer of the Bertha Capen Reynolds Society.

Preface

Inequality abounds in our society. However, nowhere is there a longer history of unequal treatment than in the relationship between Native Americans and the European colonizers of this country. From Colonial times to the present, American Indian people have been marginalized and treated unequally by the majority culture. The ramifications of this history are very real today. There is no one American Indian culture nor one experience. There are hundreds of sovereign American Indian tribal communities with diverse languages, rituals, and beliefs. In spite of this rich diversity, there is a commonality of oppression.

This volume draws together varying analyses of some of the current issues which highlight the impact of inequality and poverty of resources and opportunities. We have included analysis of the dramatic changes in public assistance through "welfare reform," and the new economic independence and strength which is emerging through the operation of American Indian gaming facilities. This collection also covers the impact of cultural changes and majority dominance as evidenced by social problems, specifically domestic violence and lack of adequate health care. The volume concludes with an examination of cultural bias, how professionals can be misguided by dominant majority ideas and consequently miss or ignore critical strengths among American Indian people and their culture.

The last three articles present the reflections of three women and their experiences with inequality. They demonstrate how injustice permeates their lives from day-to-day tasks to the fulfillment of long-term goals. Yet, in spite of oppression, there is a sense that cultural strength prevails.

[Haworth co-indexing entry note]: "Preface." Segal, Elizabeth A., and Keith M. Kilty. Co-published simultaneously in *Journal of Poverty* (The Haworth Press, Inc.) Vol. 2, No. 4, 1998, pp. xiii-xiv; and: *Pressing Issues of Inequality and American Indian Communities* (ed: Elizabeth A. Segal and Keith M. Kilty) The Haworth Press, Inc., 1998, pp. xiii-xiv. Single or multiple copies of this article are available for a fee from The Haworth Document Delivery Service [1-800-342-9678, 9:00 a.m. - 5:00 p.m. (EST). E-mail address: getinfo@haworthpressinc.com].

xiii

Taken together, these articles and reflections address some of the pressing issues facing American Indian communities today. With over 500 different American Indian tribes in the United States, the aspects of inequality faced by tribal communities are vast. This volume attempts to begin a discussion that deserves far more attention than it receives today. We hope others will continue this dialogue.

Elizabeth A. Segal
Keith M. Kilty

The Implications of "Welfare Reform" for American Indian Families and Communities

Layne K. Stromwall
Stephanie Brzuzy
Polly Sharp
Celina Andersen

SUMMARY. This paper focuses on the impact of the latest welfare reform initiatives, through the Temporary Assistance for Needy Families block grant (TANF) and its modification through the Balanced Budget Act of 1997, on Arizona American Indian families, a group disproportionately affected by poverty and lack of economic opportunity. This paper also contrasts the impact of TANF on American Indian populations living off the reservation with its impact on American Indian families living on reservations. Potential effects on tribal communities are discussed. *[Article copies available for a fee from The Haworth Document Delivery Service: 1-800-342-9678. E-mail address: getinfo@haworthpressinc.com]*

Layne K. Stromwall, PhD, is Assistant Professor, Arizona State University School of Social Work, PO Box 871802, Tempe, AZ 85287-1802.

Stephanie Brzuzy, PhD, is Assistant Professor, Arizona State University School of Social Work.

Polly Sharp, MSW, is Human Services Policy Director, Inter Tribal Council of Arizona.

Celina Andersen, BA, is a Graduate Student, Arizona State University School of Social Work.

[Haworth co-indexing entry note]: "The Implications of 'Welfare Reform' for American Indian Families and Communities." Stromwall, Layne K. et al. Co-published simultaneously in *Journal of Poverty* (The Haworth Press, Inc.) Vol. 2, No. 4, 1998, pp. 1-15; and: *Pressing Issues of Inequality and American Indian Communities* (ed: Elizabeth A. Segal and Keith M. Kilty) The Haworth Press, Inc., 1998, pp. 1-15. Single or multiple copies of this article are available for a fee from The Haworth Document Delivery Service [1-800-342-9678, 9:00 a.m. - 5:00 p.m. (EST). E-mail address: getinfo@haworthpressinc.com].

KEYWORDS. American Indian, Native American, Arizona, Temporary Assistance for Needy Families block grant (TANF), poverty, Personal Responsibility and Work Opportunity Reconciliation Act of 1996, P. L. 104-193 (PRWORA)

The campaign pledge by President Clinton in 1994 to "end welfare as we know it" set in motion a chain of events that have radically altered the provision of public assistance. While all recipients of public assistance will be affected by the legislative changes of 1996, the poorest populations and those most severely limited in employment opportunities will be most affected by these changes. Among the poorest groups in the U.S. are American Indians. Consequently, the effects of "welfare reform" may be greatest on the native people of this country.

This paper focuses on the impact of the latest reform initiatives, through the Temporary Assistance for Needy Families block grant (TANF) and its modification through the Balanced Budget Act of 1997, on Arizona American Indian families who live on and off reservations. Before the passage of the legislation that created TANF, several states were granted waivers to implement state "reform" programs. Arizona was granted a waiver and began to implement many of the changes in the new federal law in November of 1995, a year earlier than mandated by TANF. Thus, analysis of Arizona's current situation allows assessment of the initial effect of these "reform" measures earlier than in other states. Arizona's current experience provides a window to the future for other states.

Arizona has one of the largest concentrations of American Indian people in the United States, with more than 200,000 persons living on and off reservations as of 1992 (U.S. Bureau of the Census, 1996). Furthermore, according to 1990 census figures, the state of Arizona has the largest on-reservation population of American Indians, with more than 140,000 people living in Indian Country (Inter Tribal Council of Arizona, written communication, November 1997). American Indian families disproportionately experience extreme poverty conditions and require the services of public assistance programs. According to the Inter Tribal Council of Arizona (ITCA), a nonprofit organization that represents 19 tribes in Arizona, the poverty rate on Arizona reservations was 53.7% as reported in the 1990 census. Although the American Indian population in

Arizona is not quite six percent of the entire state population, almost 18% of the poverty population is American Indian (Arizona Community Action Association, Inc., 1994). Arizona's September, 1997, American Indian AFDC recipients numbered 140,079 persons, comprising 50,868 households (Arizona Department of Economic Security, 1997). More than 85% of those persons lived away from their home reservation.

In 1995, nine tribes in Arizona experienced jobless rates between 50 and 90% (U.S. Department of the Interior, Bureau of Indian Affairs, 1995). This represents almost half of all reservations in Arizona. These high poverty and jobless rates are accompanied by other problems that limit people's employability. For example, in 1997, the Salt River Pima-Maricopa Indian Community, population 5,480 (U.S. Department of the Interior, Bureau of Indian Affairs, 1995), reported an 80% dropout rate for students in grades K-12 (M. Lewis, Vice President of the Salt River Pima-Maricopa Indian Community, Public Testimony: Arizona Works Agency Procurement Board Meeting, September 18, 1997).

Because of the high levels of poverty, American Indians will be one of the most vulnerable groups affected by the mandated changes. Legislators acknowledged the poverty conditions on many reservations by including provisions in the new laws to ease the impact on tribal communities in the following ways. First, tribal governments may choose to offer their own programs. If a tribe chooses to run its own program, families living on that reservation will not fall under the state TANF requirements. Second, tribal communities with a jobless rate of more than 50% are exempt from TANF time limit requirements. Third, additional monies are available to tribes for job placement for those persons with many barriers to employment. The exemptions and additional monies benefit American Indian families who live on reservations. Based on the 1990 census, 26% of American Indian people in Arizona lived off-reservation (Arizona Community Action Association, Inc., 1994). Thus, those families who do not live on qualifying reservations are subject to state TANF requirements.[1]

This paper discusses major provisions of TANF and specific modifications enacted through the Balanced Budget Act, and the way in which their implementation in the State of Arizona has

initially affected American Indian families. This paper also contrasts the impact of TANF on American Indian populations living
off the reservation with its impact on American Indian families
living on reservations. Potential effects on tribal communities are
discussed.

FEDERAL REFORM
OF PUBLIC ASSISTANCE PROGRAMS:
THE LEGISLATION

Since 1935, Aid to Families with Dependent Children (AFDC)
had been the key federal and state cash assistance program for
families who were poor. Public assistance programs, particularly
AFDC, have become increasingly restrictive and punitive in the last
30 years. Originally, women received AFDC support to stay at
home and raise their children. However, legislative changes in recent years restricted eligibility and imposed work requirements for
adult recipients of AFDC (Abramovitz, 1996).

Assistance to families who are poor radically changed with the
enactment of the Personal Responsibility and Work Opportunity
Reconciliation Act, P.L. 104-193 (PRWORA) on August 22, 1996.
This law ends the Aid to Families with Dependent Children
(AFDC), Emergency Assistance (EA), and JOBS programs that
were based on matching grant formulas established between the
federal and state governments. The law replaces them with the
Temporary Assistance for Needy Families (TANF) block grant. The
block grant is a fixed amount of money appropriated by the federal
government to states. The TANF funds are capped through fiscal
year 2003. In order to receive full TANF block grant funds, states
must contribute at least 80% of their 1994 funding contributions for
AFDC, JOBS, EA, and child care expenditures (Katz, 1996; U.S.
Department of Health and Human Services, 1996).

This new law ends the 60-year federal guarantee of assistance for
families who are poor. The law is complex. Each state is currently
in the process of interpreting how it will be implemented in that
state. However, the Children's Defense Fund (1996) estimated that
as many as one million additional children will fall into poverty
because of this legislation.

Among its most significant provisions for families who are poor are time limits for assistance and stricter work requirements than were enacted in previous welfare reform efforts (such as the 1988 Family Support Act, P.L. 100-485). The federal TANF time limits include a maximum of five total years of cash assistance for adult recipients; however, states need not provide five consecutive years of cash assistance. TANF mandates that families must receive full benefits for two years at a time. After two years of cash assistance, states have options. Arizona has chosen to limit adult recipients to two years of cash assistance out of a five-year (60 month) period.

In addition, states must require parents to work after two years of assistance ("Points of Agreement," 1996). With the new work requirements, communities will need to develop sufficient services and infrastructure to permit parents to work. For example, the demand for additional child care services will increase. Care for infants is particularly lacking. The U.S. General Accounting Office (1997) estimated that the city of Chicago, Illinois, can provide only 14% of the needed infant care that the new work requirements will create, based on that city's current supply.

Historically, the positive or negative outcome of a public welfare policy reform initiative has been measured by a change in the number of families receiving assistance. If caseloads decreased, the policy initiative was deemed a success. Outcomes of TANF are designed to be measured in the same manner, and states will be fiscally sanctioned if they do not meet certain targeted reductions. At the end of six years, states must demonstrate caseload reduction to be eligible for full federal funding (Center for Law and Social Policy, 1996). In addition, if states reduce their caseloads according to the federal requirements, they can reduce state spending for TANF (Savner and Greenberg, 1997). Consequently, it will be in the best fiscal interest of the states to find ways to decrease caseloads and, in turn, spend less money.

This legislation has significant implications for American Indian families who are poor and for their tribal communities. As indicated above, American Indian families who are poor are among the most vulnerable groups to be affected. Exemptions from the time limits are allowed for reservations with a jobless rate of at least 50 percent. This was a major provision negotiated and passed as part of the 1997 Balanced Budget Act. In Arizona, nine reservations with an estimated population of over 114,000 persons are currently exempted. Arizona was one of the first states to immediately implement this exemption on November 1, 1997. The exemption preserves cash assistance for more than 80% of families on reservations who would have seen a reduction in benefits. However, families living on exempted reservations who are out of compliance with work requirements can potentially lose all of their benefits if they are sanctioned.

The new legislation will change the structure of public assistance for tribes in many ways. In one significant change, tribes can opt to set up their own programs, resulting in more flexibility and exemptions than state TANF programs currently allow. However, these policies will not affect urban and rural American Indian families who do not live on reservations.[2] They will be subject to the state TANF requirements. To date, three tribes in Arizona, White Mountain Apache, Pascua Yaqui, and Navajo, have elected to run their own programs. However, regulations for the operation of these programs are still being negotiated, and the Balanced Budget Act of 1997 made new changes to the reform initiatives, further complicating implementation. In addition, states have the option of providing state match money to tribes who agree to run their own programs. The Arizona legislature has agreed to supply match money to tribes who choose to run their own programs.

UNFOLDING IMPACT
ON AMERICAN INDIAN FAMILIES IN ARIZONA

The time limits and sanctions that recently took effect in Arizona are already having a significant impact on American Indian families. This analysis is based on current implementation of the legislative changes, acknowledging that many details remain to be decided. While time limits and sanctions will affect many families in Arizona, American Indian families face unique circumstances due to poverty, lack of employment opportunities, and discrimination that disproportionately affect their ability to provide for family well-being. For example, Ronnie Lupe, the chairman of the White Mountain Apache Tribe, states,

As the leader of the White Mountain Apache Tribe, which has an unemployment rate of at least 35%,[3] this law gives me grave concern. In my opinion, it is a perfect reflection of the perception that the dominant society has of the welfare community. That is, that those who are on welfare are perfectly capable of working, and at the snap of the fingers could enter the work force. Of course, how people find jobs when no jobs are available is an issue not addressed in the legislation. This is not only naive but basically mean spirited . . . The White Mountain Apache Tribe did not create welfare, the federal government did. So if it's the federal government's intent to dismantle welfare, then it should provide opportunities for welfare recipients rather than throwing them out on the street. (Lupe, 1996, p. 2)

The Impact of Time Limits and Sanctions

American Indians who live on reservations comprise approximately 15-18% of the AFDC/TANF caseloads in Arizona. In June 1997, this represented 20,930 individuals, of whom 6,867 were adults and 14,063 were children (personal communication, Department of Economic Security, October, 1997). Individual families receiving assistance are affected by new requirements and regulations concerning not only compliance with work-related requirements, but also an overall time limit on receipt of assistance. While states have many options to implement federal time limits, Arizona has opted to allow TANF to be provided to parents only during two years out of a five-year period. However, children continue to receive benefits if the parent meets work requirements. Exemptions from the 24-month time period for the parent may be granted on a month-by-month basis for a number of reasons, among them the parent's mental or physical disability, need to care for a disabled household member, participation in a subsidized job program, or status as a victim of domestic violence (Department of Economic Security, personal communication, October 31, 1997). Thus, a parent who has previously received assistance for 24 months may continue to receive it if she can prove that she qualifies for any of the exemptions, but she must provide proof each month.

At the same time, a family can lose all cash benefits (for both parent and children) if the parent fails to comply with the work-related requirements. Twenty-five percent of benefits are lost during the first month, 50 percent the second month, and 100 percent the third month. In Arizona, parents were notified of this major structural change in requirements by letter, indicating that recipients needed to immediately visit their TANF caseworker for assignment to a three-week work preparation class. If the parent did not respond or could not reply, the increasing sanctions were imposed over three months. In Arizona, 1324 of approximately 5500 TANF recipients receiving letters responded; thus 4,176 were potentially sanctioned (Kossan, 1997). If a sanctioned parent later complies with requirements, confirmation is required to reestablish full benefits.

Case Examples Illustrating Potential Impacts

The disproportionate impact on American Indian families will be felt in different ways in urban areas and Indian Country. The following case examples are composites constructed from the application of new regulations to family situations and do not represent actual families. The composites are based on the authors' discussions with Arizona caseworkers who are currently implementing the changes. The case examples and accompanying analysis provide a means of describing the current and projected overall impact on American Indian families. This allows a change of focus to individual families and away from a focus on success measured through reduction in caseloads. The effect of residence in an urban area is contrasted with residence on reservations. Two women, Anna and Louella, have identical situations except for their place of residence. The children's fathers are not involved in their care and support. Both fathers live on their respective reservations, where the State does not have jurisdiction to enforce legal child support.

American Indian Families Living in Urban Areas

Anna is a single mother of three living off her home reservation in a large Southwestern city. Anna lost her personal TANF benefit on November 1, 1997, because she had already received benefits for two years under Arizona's public assistance program. Two of

Anna's three children continue to receive TANF benefits of approximately $216.00 per month because Anna is in compliance with work requirements. Anna's third child was born after Arizona's waiver program took effect on November 1, 1995. In the state-implemented waiver program, children born into families already receiving benefits did not qualify for increased cash assistance for the new baby. Anna and her family remain eligible for health care, child care, WIC, and food stamps, and live in subsidized public housing.

Anna, who has a ninth-grade education, complies with work requirements by attending the JOBS program and by looking for work. Child care is provided when Anna is in training and when she seeks work. Anna has completed 30 job applications, most of them for minimum wage jobs, in the last two weeks. Some of the jobs would require her to travel long distances by public transportation. Since the public transportation system is very poor in her area, she is worried that she cannot get to some job locations.

Due to her reduced budget, Anna was unable to pay her full utility bill at the end of November. She knows she is at risk of eviction from public housing if she falls behind in her utility payments. Anna applied for twenty more jobs this week, but has received no job offers. She has no savings with which to move to a new location in the city.

Anna thinks of moving back in with family on her home reservation unless she finds work soon. Her reservation has more than a 50% jobless rate, so she would be eligible for TANF for herself as well as her children if she lived there.

American Indian Families Living on Reservations

Louella is a twenty-year-old single mother of three children living on her home reservation in rural Arizona. Because her tribe qualifies for an exemption from TANF time limits due to its documented jobless rate of more than 50%, Louella's TANF benefits did not change November 1, 1997, even though she had already received benefits for two years under Arizona's cash assistance program. Louella and two of her three children receive $288 per month because Louella meets work requirements. Louella's third child was born after November 1, 1995, while Louella was already receiving assistance, making the family ineligible for an increased payment based on that child. The family continues to be eligible for health care, child care, WIC, and food stamps. They live in subsidized tribal housing.

Although her tribe is exempted from time limits, Louella must continue to comply with work-related requirements to maintain her family's eligibility for assistance. Louella, who has a ninth-grade education, complies by attending the JOBS program. She has applied at five local businesses, but none have actual positions available.

Comparison

Anna and Louella have identical histories; only their current place of residence differs. Anna's monthly income is $72.00 less than Louella receives because Louella lives on a reservation exempt from TANF time limits. That relatively small amount is enough to interfere with her already-tight budget. As a result, Anna cannot pay her full utility bill. Anna knows that as a resident of public housing, she must keep current on her utility payments or risk eviction.

Anna has little education and few job skills. Thus, she is competitive only for the lowest-paying jobs. She must remain in compliance with work-related requirements to maintain her children's benefits, but she is unlikely to secure a job that will support herself and her children. At the same time, she is struggling to maintain her family's status with a 25% reduction in a monthly budget already well below the poverty level, a situation that often begins a family's slide into homelessness. Like many families in this situation, she will turn to family and friends for shelter, and these family and friends reside on her home reservation.

In comparison, Louella and her family are not at immediate risk due to her tribe's exemption from time limits. However, she believes there is little chance of obtaining a job in her home community due to the already high unemployment rate, whether or not she gains skills through education and training. If she moves away from the reservation, she loses her exemption. If she remains on her home reservation, even after she gains job skills, she may not have the opportunity to use them except through unpaid community service.

DISCUSSION AND IMPLICATIONS

The legislative changes have created additional pressure for American Indian families in need of cash assistance. Families living in urban areas, who have exhausted the two-year time limit, may be unable to survive financially with the reduction in benefits. If they move back to their reservations to share resources with family, there will be additional pressure on those extended families and on tribal and related services, including housing, education and health care.

Housing on reservations is already limited in amount and quality. Many reservations lack sufficient housing for the families already residing there. Particularly, subsidized tribal housing is currently unable to serve all tribal members who request it. In 1990, two HUD programs in Indian Country, the Rental Program and the Mutual Help lease-purchase program, accounted for 26 percent of all American Indian households and 42 percent of those with low incomes (Urban Institute, 1996).

Therefore, when families move back to the reservation, often the only housing available will be to move in with extended family. A study of the housing status of American Indians by the Urban Institute (1996) estimated that forty percent of American Indians living on reservations lived in substandard housing. The study also found that tribal areas closer to urban centers had smaller percentages of households living in substandard housing, suggesting that more remote reservations struggled to a greater extent with a lack of utilities and the infrastructure needed to provide plumbing and electricity.

Education systems serving reservations will be greatly stressed. Tribal colleges, like community colleges, will face increased pressure to admit many more students who need training due to participation in TANF work requirements. According to Shanley (1997), tribal colleges will face shortages in facilities, instructors and child care on campus and in the community. Currently, tribal colleges prepare students to further their education. Tribal colleges do not receive federal funds for providing GED programs or for basic and remedial adult education, which will be greatly needed for TANF recipients. In addition, the legislative changes focus only on short-term training programs. Training programs lasting more than one year are not considered work-related and therefore do not exempt an individual from work requirements. For individuals, like many American Indian parents, who enter the system with a low level of educational attainment, short-term training will not be sufficient to remediate basic skills, much less gain an occupational skill that can result in a job that pays a living wage.

Education within public schools serving reservation residents will also be stressed. Since parental TANF recipients under age 18 who are not high school graduates must stay in school to comply with work requirements, school districts serving them will see an increased need for specialized programs for pregnant and parenting students. Issues of transportation, often from rural reservation locales to large regional high schools, must be addressed for young parents as well as their children.

While the Balanced Budget Act of 1997 created an important exemption for tribes with 50% or more jobless rates, the exemption is not without future ramifications. Pressures on these tribes' services may increase if their urban members cannot survive away from their home reservation due to loss of TANF benefits. In addition, the exemptions do not apply to work requirements, so tribes must provide additional child care, remedial education and adult education. Without economic development and job creation, tribes will find it difficult to train and place recipients in jobs.

Decreased caseloads may be interpreted as a success for the taxpayer, but they are not always the result of a success for families. The legislative changes will result in decreased caseloads for many reasons described in this paper. These include the sanctioning of families out of compliance with work requirements and the imposition of time limits on cash assistance as well as parents obtaining work. Analysis of the outcomes for families who have left the rolls because they found work reveals a dismal picture. For example, job placement outcomes to date indicate a preponderance of low-wage, service industry positions with little chance of advancement. During fiscal year 1997, the Arizona Department of Economic Security reports that 7400 TANF recipients found work at an average hourly wage of $5.98 (Blessing, 1997). Whether these parents are working full-time (i.e., working sufficient hours to maintain a living wage) is unknown. They may only be working enough hours to meet the legislative requirements of 20 hours per week for parents of children under the age of six and 30 hours per week for parents of older children. While former TANF recipients maintain their health and child care benefits for two years under the legislative changes in Arizona (the federal law requires a minimum of one year), the jobs TANF recipients are securing are historically not the type of employment that provides job advancement at an increasing wage or includes employer-provided fringe benefits. Thus, within five years the family will exhaust cash assistance and will need to survive on the hourly wage alone.

While we have some knowledge of what happens to families who find work, we have very limited knowledge of what happens to families who are sanctioned for lack of compliance with work-related requirements, or who lose benefits because they have exhausted time limits on assistance. Efforts need to be made to determine the status and quality of life of families who are a part of caseload reduction. Arizona's welfare reform legislation included provisions to evaluate the effects on families, but this effort has not yet been implemented. Other evaluation efforts are planned.

This paper has described reasons why American Indian families are disproportionately affected by the legislative changes. Low levels of educational attainment upon entry to the public assistance system, historic poverty conditions within the extended family, and economic conditions in Indian Country are factors that make it more difficult for American Indian families to be successful in the "one size fits all" TANF program.

CONCLUSION

If the intent of "welfare reform" was to create more work opportunities and a greater sense of personal responsibility for recipients, it seems unlikely that these outcomes will be achieved in Indian communities without extensive economic development efforts that include sustainable wage jobs and adequate family supports. The effects of the complex provisions and subsequent implementation of welfare reform legislation will continue to unfold as families move in and out of compliance with TANF regulations and exhaust their time-limited benefits. To determine the effects of these changes, it is critical that the real impact on families and their communities, not just the aggregate reporting of caseloads, be monitored. Without knowledge of the effects on the real lives of families, it may be easy to say that welfare reform "works" because caseloads are reduced and the cost of that program appears less. What is less easy to ascertain are the effects on families, particularly American Indian families, whose residence, background and preparation impact on their ability to find employment in areas where few job opportunities are available.

NOTES

1. The Pascua Yaqui, a tribe of 11,060 persons, has opted to administer their own TANF program and will serve tribal members on and off their reservation.
2. See Note 1.
3. According to the Bureau of Indian Affairs, more than 50% (U.S. Department of the Interior, 1995).

REFERENCES

Abramovitz, M. (1996). *Regulating the lives of women* (revised ed.). Boston MA: South End Press.

Arizona Community Action Association, Inc. (1994). *Poverty in Arizona: A shared responsibility: Addressing the needs of Arizona's poor.* Phoenix, AZ: Author.

Arizona Department of Economic Security, (1997). *AFDC households and recipients by reservation (tribe).* Phoenix, AZ: Author.

Blessing, L.J. (1997). "Changes work well–so far," *Arizona Republic*, November 2, 1997, pp. H1-H2.

Center for Law and Public Policy. (1996). *The welfare bill's work requirements.* Washington, DC: Author.

Children's Defense Fund. (1996, August 1). *Action alert: President Clinton betrays America's children* [On-line]. HN3208@handsnet.org.

Inter Tribal Council of Arizona. (1997, August). *Welfare reform in Indian country: Fact sheet.* Phoenix, AZ: Author.

Inter Tribal Council of Arizona. (1997, June). *Welfare reform in Indian country: Fact sheet.* Phoenix, AZ: Author.

Inter Tribal Council of Arizona (1990). *1990 Profile of American Indian tribes.* Phoenix, AZ: Author.

Katz, J.L. (1996). After 60 years, most control is passing to states: Clinton will sign measure requiring recipients to work and setting time limit on benefits. *Congressional Quarterly, 54,* 2190-2196.

Kossan, P. (1997). Welfare cuts kick in: Some Arizona moms lose 25%, fear for kids. *Arizona Republic*, October 15, A1.

Lupe, R. (1996). Chairman's corner: If the welfare reform act remains as it is, human misery is certain to follow. *Fort Apache Scout*.

Points of agreement, and disagreement, on the welfare bill. (1996, August 1). *The New York Times*, p. A8.

Savner, S. and Greenberg, M. (1997, March). *The new framework: Alternative state funding choices under TANF*. Washington, DC: Center for Law and Social Policy.

Shanley, J. (1997). Welfare reform and the tribal colleges: Who's left holding the bag? *Tribal College Journal*, Spring, 1997.

U.S. Department of Health and Human Services. (1996). *Summary of provisions: Personal Responsibility and Work Opportunity Act of 1996 (H.R. 3734)*. Washington, DC: Author.

U.S. Department of the Interior, Bureau of Indian Affairs, (1995). *Indian service population and labor force estimates*. Washington, DC: Author.

U.S. General Accounting Office. (1997). *Welfare reform: Implications of increased work participation for child care* (GAO Publication No. HEHS 97-75). Washington, DC: US Government Printing Office.

Urban Institute (1996). American Indian housing. *Policy and research report, 26* (1), 7-15.

The Impact of Indian Gaming on Economic Development

Karen Gerdes
Maria Napoli
Clinton M. Pattea
Elizabeth A. Segal

SUMMARY. Over the past ten years, gaming on Indian reservations has become a source of tremendous economic development. The impact of gaming has been to dramatically change the social, political and economic state of numerous American Indian communities. This article presents a policy analysis of the impact of Indian gaming nationally and highlights one community, the Fort McDowell Yavapai Reservation in central Arizona. *[Article copies available for a fee from The Haworth Document Delivery Service: 1-800-342-9678. E-mail address: getinfo@haworthpressinc.com]*

KEYWORDS. Gaming, economic development, American Indian, community development, casinos

Karen Gerdes, PhD, is Assistant Professor, Arizona State University School of Social Work, PO Box 871802, Tempe, AZ 85287-1802.

Maria Napoli, PhD, is Assistant Professor, Arizona State University School of Social Work, PO Box 871802, Tempe, AZ 85287-1802.

Clinton M. Pattea, BS, is President of the Tribal Council at Fort McDowell Yavapai Reservation, Fort McDowell, AZ.

Elizabeth A. Segal, PhD, is Professor, Arizona State University School of Social Work, PO Box 871802, Tempe, AZ 85287-1802.

[Haworth co-indexing entry note]: "The Impact of Indian Gaming on Economic Development." Gerdes, Karen et al. Co-published simultaneously in *Journal of Poverty* (The Haworth Press, Inc.) Vol. 2, No. 4, 1998, pp. 17-30; and: *Pressing Issues of Inequality and American Indian Communities* (ed: Elizabeth A. Segal and Keith M. Kilty) The Haworth Press, Inc., 1998, pp. 17-30. Single or multiple copies of this article are available for a fee from The Haworth Document Delivery Service [1-800-342-9678, 9:00 a.m. - 5:00 p.m. (EST). E-mail address: getinfo@haworthpressinc.com].

17

Gambling and betting on games of chance often evoke the image of sleazy backroom dealings, illegal activities, or compulsive behaviors that bankrupt people. While gambling has its "dark" side, for American Indian communities there is another perspective. Over the past ten years, gaming on Indian reservations has become a source of tremendous economic development. The impact of gaming has been to dramatically change the social, political and economic state of numerous American Indian communities. This article presents a policy analysis of the impact of Indian gaming nationally and highlights one community, the Fort McDowell Yavapai Reservation in central Arizona.

The political history of American Indian tribes in this country has been characterized by shifting positions on the part of the Federal government. The Federal government has treated American Indian communities at times as autonomous sovereign states and at other times as wards of the state to be taken care of and controlled. The shifts between these two positions seem to have followed a pattern: when American Indian tribes possessed something wanted or needed by the federal government, intervention and control were used and treaties were signed. When American Indians were perceived to have little to offer and were in need of social and economic support, sovereignty and self-sufficiency seemed to be encouraged. What these two positions have created is a pattern of government entities taking when there is something to take, and ignoring American Indian communities when there is some need. This pattern can be seen through analysis of some of the major federal policies towards American Indians.

WARDS OF THE STATE

Early colonists had come to this country to stake claims to land for themselves and their home countries. The native people were a problem to be removed. The settlers "had little use for Indians. The Indians were 'savages' (being hunters) and 'devil worshippers' (not being Christians); they were nuisances who blocked the growth of this new English-speaking colonial world" (Nabokov, 1992, p. 20).

Before the development of the West, major public policies concerning Indians did not exist. Local treaties were used to control tribes, and most treaties were handled by the Bureau of Indian Affairs (BIA) which was developed in 1824 under the Department of the Interior (Segal & Brzuzy, 1998). Because of the large expanses of land, the American Indian tribes could be pushed further west without the need for large-scale government intervention. American Indians were treated as small bands, from whom land could simply be taken.

> When invading Europeans, hungry for ownership of land they couldn't get in their native Europe, made their genocidal sweep across what was to them newly 'discovered' territory, they drove Native Americans from what they saw as the best and richest portions onto reservations. But over that land the invaders viewed as the least valuable, Native Americans were granted limited sovereignty. (Lane, 1995, p. 21)

Westward expansion created the need for broader policies for Indian containment. It was no longer easy to simply take land. In 1886, the Supreme court ruled that Indian tribes were "wards of the nation" and as such were dependent on the United States (Nabokov, 1992). By denying American Indians sovereignty, the Federal government could take over control of Indian affairs. This paved the way for passage of the Dawes Act in 1887.

Congress enacted the Dawes Act in 1887 to contain American Indian populations. The Act limited the amount of land each head of an Indian family could own to 160 acres (Jansson, 1997). The impact of this law was to force tribes to break into family units, contain the amount of land each family controlled, and provide a way for outsiders to buy the land from individuals. The Dawes Act created a legal way for whites to acquire Indian land, through purchase from individuals. From 1887 to 1934, two-thirds of Indian land was taken from American Indians (Nabokov, 1992). By the 1930s, American Indians were economically destitute, living on parcels of land with minimal resources.

TRIBAL SOVEREIGNTY AND SELF-GOVERNMENT

Congressional support of sovereignty and tribal self-government emerged through passage of the Indian Reorganization Act of 1934

(O'Brian, 1989). This legislation allowed for the establishment of tribal constitutional governments. Although lack of funding and continued authority of the BIA prevented major progress towards self-sufficiency, this legislation marked the beginning of a period of self-control in exchange for minimal federal government economic support.

Tribal sovereignty was furthered through passage of the Self-Determination and Education Assistance Act of 1975. This legislation provided federal funding for tribal programs with planning and administration by the tribes. This law was strengthened through other legislation including the Indian Child Welfare Act which gave autonomy to American Indian tribes.

While tribal autonomy grew from the 1930s to the 1980s, it has come without economic independence (McCulloch, 1994). Tribal autonomy has been supported by law, but resources from the federal government have been minimal and primarily for bare minimum needs. Unemployment and poverty have been extremely high on reservations. In 1991, 30% of all American Indian households had incomes below the poverty line, with almost 40% of all Indian children below the poverty line (Reddy, 1995). Seventy-five percent of the American Indian workforce earn less than $7,000 per year with an average unemployment rate of 45% on reservations (Russell, 1995).

THE IMPACT OF SHIFTING POLICIES

The result of federal policies from the 1800s through most of the 1900s was twofold. Land and resources were stripped away through early policies of control and containment of tribes as "wards of the state." Then, when tribal sovereignty was achieved, it came with a price–no resources or means for significant economic autonomy and reservations on poor land. Before gaming, tribes relied heavily on federal support. The ironic situation of gaining recognition of sovereignty while struggling financially was evident during the 1980s:

> Despite President Reagan's apparent support for tribal sovereignty, which he characterized as a 'government to govern-

ment' relationship, Indian program funding suffered severe budget cuts under his administration . . . The build-up of federally funded economic and social programs on the reservations during the 1970s left the tribal economies particularly vulnerable to the Reagan-era budget cuts. (Wilkins & Ritter, 1994, pp. 309-310)

The tragic irony for American Indians was that when they had resources, they were to be controlled, and when they no longer had those resources, they were left on their own. Either way represented a loss for the Indian people. This pattern is now being challenged with the advent of gaming and casinos on American Indian reservations.

THE HISTORY OF INDIAN GAMING

Games of chance, while not new, began to proliferate in the late 1970s and early 1980s. Non-profit groups were turning to bingo as a way to raise funds for their efforts. Many state governments began to use lotteries as a way to generate extra revenues. At the same time, Indian tribes began to operate bingo halls. As sovereign nations, Indian tribes were free to manage affairs on tribal land with minimal interference, and the tribes argued that this included gaming (National Indian Gaming Association, 1995).

In general, sovereignty means that tribal governments are authorized to govern within the limits of federal and state criminal laws. State civil laws are not binding unless accepted by the tribal authorities. Tribes have their own civil laws and are responsible for enforcing those laws. In most states, gaming such as bingo, lotteries, and casino nights for non-profit fundraising fall under civil law. As such, if games were held on tribal land, then the proceedings would fall under sovereign Indian rule, not state civil laws.

Legal action pushed the issue of gaming on reservations. In 1979, state courts ruled that the Seminole Tribe in Florida could run high stakes bingo games (Munting, 1996). The decision was appealed, and after a 1982 Supreme Court ruling upholding tribal sovereignty, Indian-sponsored bingo games proliferated. The Court ruled that if bingo was legal elsewhere in the state, states could not prohibit bingo on Indian reservations, and states could not regulate it due to sovereignty (Angle, 1988). This ruling was upheld in 1987 through the case California v. Cabazon and Morongo Bands, 480 U.S. 202. After seven years of struggling to gain the right to operate a gaming facility, the small Cabazon tribe of California won the right through the courts (Lane, 1995). Through this landmark decision, the Supreme Court ruled if states already allowed forms of gaming, such gaming on Indian reservations could not be regulated by state and local governments.

While states had challenged tribal rights to operate bingo halls, the proliferation of these enterprises and the level of financial profits created a stronger will for state regulation. Anders (1996) summed up the sentiment of state officials in regard to Indian gaming: "It is okay for tribes to do something to help their people, but they should not get in the way of established interests" (p. 84). Wilkins and Ritter (1994) in their analysis of gaming in the Midwest agreed with this sentiment and attributed it to the newfound income for tribes: "Since Indian gaming left untaxed revenue within state boundaries, the states were not willing to give up their attempts to regulate" (p. 311).

THE INDIAN GAMING REGULATORY ACT OF 1988

Congress, after the Cabazon Tribe case, actively engaged in debate to regulate gaming on Indian reservations. The Indian Gaming Regulatory Act (IGRA) was passed in 1988 to create a framework for negotiations between tribes and states and create a system of oversight (General Accounting Office, 1997; Eadington, 1996). The IGRA states that states must negotiate in good faith with tribes, and if they do not, the tribes can go to federal courts for mediation or arbitration. The law also categorizes gaming into three classes: Class I which includes social gaming for nominal prizes; Class II which includes bingo; and Class III which includes casino games, slot machines, and pari-mutuel betting. Class III gaming has tended to be the area of greatest conflict between states and tribes, as well as the level of games which generates the greatest amount of spending.

Because the Supreme Court, followed by Congress, upheld the right of American Indian tribes to run gaming facilities on their reservations, the area of contention shifted. It no longer was a struggle of whether gaming would be allowed, now it became an issue of how many casinos there could be in a state, where they could be located, and who would profit (Eadington, 1996). The IGRA specified that tribes and state must enter into a compact that balances the interests of both parties, and that the net revenues from gaming must be used to fund tribal government operations, or provide for the general welfare of the tribal members, or promote tribal economic development, or donate to charitable organizations, or fund efforts of local government agencies (U.S. General Accounting Office, 1987).

The Indian Gaming Regulatory Act of 1988, while allowing tribes to operate gaming facilities, established rules and regulations which placed controls on tribal sovereignty. This policy fits the historical pattern of U.S. government relations with Indian tribes: when the American Indian people have resources, tribal sovereignty is curtailed. In spite of the constraints of the IGRA, tribes that have managed to develop a gaming compact with their state government have economically benefited from the casinos.

THE DEVELOPMENTAL IMPACT OF INDIAN GAMING

Over the past twenty years, legalized gambling has proliferated throughout the United States. While the most common forms of gambling are state lotteries, racetracks, and bingo, Indian gaming has gained a significant presence within the industry. In 1976, only Nevada and New Jersey allowed casino gambling. Today, casino gambling is legal in 23 states, and of those, 20 allow tribal casinos (Kaye, 1996). As of December 31, 1996, 184 tribes operated 281 gaming facilities, representing 55% of all continental U.S. tribes (U.S. General Accounting Office, 1997). Based on the General Accounting Office survey of 178 of the facilities, the Indian gaming facilities generated about 10% of the gaming revenues generated by legalized gambling in 1995. The largest share of gaming revenue, 40%, was generated by non-Indian casinos, while 34% of the revenue was through lotteries. Pari-mutuel betting generated about 8% of the revenue, and the rest came from charitable games and bingo.

Indian gaming is a small part of the entire gaming industry, just ten percent. However, for Indian Class III facilities, the share amounted to almost four billion dollars in 1995. The majority of this revenue was generated by 13% of the Class III gaming facilities. Almost sixty percent of the revenue was shared by 15 major Class III facilities (U.S. General Accounting Office, 1997). Although the bulk of the income has been concentrated among a minority of the tribes, the economic impact has been significant. For those tribes where the income has not been as high, the benefits have still been significant. For many of these tribes, gaming has brought the only new economic opportunity for the reservation. For example, for the Cabazon, before gaming there was absolutely nothing on tribal land–"no facilities, no water, no development whatsoever, just dry desert land" (Lane, 1996, p. 180). As a result of gaming, not only is there a large gaming facility, but 17 custom homes and a nearby environmentally safe power plant that is anchoring a new industrial park have been built. There are a number of key areas where gaming has benefited American Indian tribes.

Job Creation

The National Indian Gaming Association reports that gaming has put 140,000 people to work in jobs related to the gaming industry on reservations (Kaye, 1996). As of 1993, more than 2100 jobs had been created in San Diego County by the Sycuan Tribe Gaming Center. The Center is the largest minority-owned employer in San Diego county and generated $70 million in 1993 alone (McGladrey & Pullen, 1993).

Two casinos on the Gila River reservation south of Phoenix employ a work force of about 1,300 employees, and more than 90% of these workers are Indians (Anders, 1996).

The Oneida Nation in upstate New York employs 1,500 workers at its casino. The U.S. Bureau of Economic Analysis multipliers for Oneida County indicate that these jobs created by the Nation indirectly create an additional 1,800 jobs within the state (Coopers & Lybrand, 1995).

Economic Gains

The Pequot Tribe in Connecticut serves more than 40,000 visitors a day who spend up to a million dollars each day (Munting,

1996). In Minnesota, dependence on public assistance dropped in those counties with Indian gaming. While other Minnesota counties experienced increases in use of public assistance, the counties with gaming had a 16% decrease (Conboy, Erkkila, & Harger, 1994). In 1993, the eight gaming facilities in Michigan paid more than $11 million in state and federal taxes, up almost 200% from the previous two years (University Associates, 1994).

Political Clout

The amounts of revenue that many of the gaming facilities have generated have elevated the tribes to become political forces. Many tribes, forced to organize and lobby in order to gain state compacts for gaming, have maintained that political organization. Consequently, many of the tribes have begun to get involved on a political level. For example, in Arizona, in an effort to force the state to develop new compacts with tribes that had not entered into gaming, tribal efforts were able to garner enough signatures to put forth an initiative to be voted during the general elections held in November of 1996. The initiative was necessary because the governor claimed that in spite of the IGRA, the state had a right to limit the number of contracts. By an overwhelming majority, 70% of the voters in Arizona approved a measure which allows tribes without gaming contracts to enter into negotiations with the state. This level of citizen support was in part due to the excellent political organization that went into the promotion of the measure.

THE YAVAPAI TRIBE OF FORT MCDOWELL

Many of the Indian tribes operating casinos have been successful in turning around economic, political and social inequality through the success of gaming. The Fort McDowell Yavapai tribe is an excellent case example of how gaming has facilitated the true meaning of tribal sovereignty and economic development. Additionally, the very inception of gaming at Fort McDowell represented a political tour de force which energized tribes across the nation (Yoder, 1995).

Following passage of the IGRA in 1988, the Yavapai of Fort McDowell prepared to open a Class III gaming facility. The regulations of the IGRA were not clear, and many tribes proceeded to open facilities, even though negotiations were not concluded. Arguing that the state was not operating in good faith, the tribe filed a law suit against the state in 1991 (Yoder, 1995).

In spite of the IGRA and the fact that the tribe (among others in the state) was already operating gaming centers, the governor refused to negotiate a compact. In May of 1992, the governor and the office of the U.S. Attorney raided the five Indian casinos, including Fort McDowell. While the state officials were able to remove all the gaming machines at the other casinos, at Fort McDowell the response was different. Residents blocked the vans and brought the state effort to a standstill. With national media attention and public interest piqued, the tribe had created a public relations problem for the governor. Public opinion supported the tribes' efforts, and two weeks after the stand-off, the governor began compact negotiations. By June of 1993, gaming compacts had been signed, although controversy and differences between the state and the tribes continue today (Yoder, 1995).

Since 1993 when the gaming compact was signed, the Yavapai tribe of Fort McDowell has experienced tremendous economic, political, and social development and an overall increase in tribal sovereignty.

The tribal casino employs 1200 people, 70% of whom are non-Indian. Jobs at the casino include 100% of medical benefits paid and in addition to salary, the casino puts 10% in a pension plan. The payroll is almost $25 million per year. About 12,000 people visit the casino daily, most of whom are from the neighboring communities. In 1996, the casino netted $90 million in profits.

Each year the Tribal Council, the governing body of the tribe, has an annual budget of $35 million for public projects. The tribe is small, with 850 members. There is a strong commitment among the tribal members to share the proceeds directly. Consequently, each member of the tribe receives a per capita allotment, which averages about $36,000 annually per person before taxes.

The impact, in addition to financial security for individual members, has been extensive. The reservation recently opened a new medical facility and community recreation center. The police force increased from five officers to a force with 26 personnel and top quality support equipment. The tribe owns a service station, farm, and a sand and gravel company. People are moving back to the reservation. Thirty to forty houses are built each year, with a waiting list of almost 130. The progress towards building is slow because of the need to also build the infrastructure to support housing and other buildings. The tribe has opened a preschool, an early years grade school, and a full social and mental health services facility. During the spring of 1997, the tribe committed one million dollars over three years to the state universities for scholarships for minority students. All of these efforts are some of the direct results of gaming on the reservation.

In addition, the financial growth has created new challenges which the Tribe is now facing. Tribal members must now learn financial management skills. This is an area the Tribal Council has yet to address and will need to in the future.

For the people of Fort McDowell, the impact of gaming has been to radically change their lives. While there are still social problems and difficulties in making the transition from poverty to economic security, the choices and opportunities available to tribal members have opened a new way of life. Below, several tribal members describe the impact of gaming from their own experience.

A 29-year-old Yavapai man and the father of two boys states:

> Gaming has afforded my family the opportunity to enjoy things in life such as traveling and having comforts in our home, like new furniture. There are many educational opportunities offered to adults and children. For example, all children may have a computer installed in their home to enhance their studies at the tribe's expense. The benefits of gaming in general have offered the Yavapai people a time to relax and enjoy life when there have been so many years of struggle in the past.

A 59-year-old Yavapai man who has served on the Tribal Council views gaming as a way to free people from financial hardship:

The values of success in Indian life is the family support system. The important things in life are free, like throwing rocks in the river with my son, spending quality time together. Gaming only gives us the opportunity to have more of that time freely.

A 35-year-old mother and educator confirms that gaming has enhanced her living style:

I can put more effort into my work and the children I serve, not having to worry about finances. Gaming money has made me more aware of how my children's lives will be since their money will be available to them when they are ready for college. They have opportunity to choose their careers and are being educated as to how to manage their money in regard to saving for the future and using it when needed. It is less stressful to know that surviving is not our purpose, living where we can maintain our traditions and still be comfortable not to worry about food and shelter. [Before gaming] when my husband was working and our income was lower, sometimes we only had $35 left to spend in the week, I was embarrassed and did not want to go to my family for money. We struggled in those times and now we can live and enjoy our work, our children and our families.

A 30-year-old father of three describes his childhood as follows:

Dad worked a job that only provided the basic necessities for the family. We did not have luxuries, such as many toys or traveling. We focused on things that did not cost money.

For him, gaming has provided opportunities:

The casino provides employment for tribal members, in fact they work and live in the same community staying close to home and family. I worked as a security guard, and then as a coin racker. Now I work as a teacher's assistant with small children in the Day School [on the reservation] and I hope to complete my BA in education. Gaming is helping to develop the reservation for future generations so that they have a place that provides jobs and income for their families, new homes, recreation for their children, their own school where they maintain tribal traditions, and keeping children in the community where they do not have to travel long distances.

CONCLUSION

For centuries, the American Indian people have lost economic, political, and social resources and rights in this country. In spite of a national policy of sovereignty, federal and state governments have regulated the lives of the Indian people. However, today gaming offers an opportunity for economic development and hence enhanced sovereignty for Indian tribes. Like other historical opportunities for resources, the American Indian people have had to struggle to keep what is rightfully theirs. So too must they struggle to continue to be allowed to pursue economic independence. Gambling and casinos are a right for entrepreneurs all over the country, including those in Las Vegas, Atlantic City, and riverboats on the Mississippi. Numerous state governments legally operate lotteries and almost every state allows horse racing. Therefore, we must ask how allowing American Indian tribes to operate gaming facilities is any different from the rights of these other entrepreneurs. The fight against the sovereign right of tribes to operate gaming is one more example of the organized efforts of state and federal governments to limit the freedoms of the American Indian people.

REFERENCES

Anders, G.C. (1996). The Indian Gaming Regulatory Act and Native American development. *International Policy Review, 6* (1), pp. 84-90.

Angle, M. (1988). Congress clears legislation to regulate Indian gambling. *Congressional Quarterly Weekly Report,* 46 (40), p. 2730.

Conboy, R.T., Erkkila, J.E., & Harger, B.T. (1994). *An economic and political analysis of Native American gaming policies.* Sault Ste. Marie, MI: Tribe of Chippewa Indians Economic Development Commission.

Coopers & Lybrand L.L.P. (1995). *An analysis of the economic impact of the Oneida Nation's presence in Oneida and Madison counties.* New York: Author.

Eadington, W.R. (1996). Ethical and policy considerations in the spread of commercial gambling. In *Gambling cultures*, Ed. J. McMillen, London: Routledge, pp. 243-262.

Kaye, M.W. (1996). Smooth sailing is expected for gambling commission. *Congressional Quarterly Weekly Report*, 54 (29), pp. 2053-2055.

Lane, A.I. (1995). *Return of the buffalo: The story behind America's Indian gaming explosion*. Westport, CT: Bergin & Garvey.

McCulloch, A.M. (1994). The politics of Indian gaming: Tribe/state relations and American federalism. *Publius: The Journal of Federalism, 24*, pp. 99-110.

McGladrey & Pullen, CPAs (1993). *The economic impact of the Sycuan Gaming Center on East San Diego County*. San Diego, CA: Author.

Munting, R. (1996). *An economic and social history of gambling in Britain and the USA*. New York, NY: Manchester University Press.

National Indian Gaming Association (1995). *Speaking the truth about Indian gaming*. National Congress of American Indians and Author.

O'Brien, S. (1989). *American Indian Tribal Governments*. Norman, OK: University of Oklahoma Press.

Russell, G. (1995). *American Indian Digest: Facts about today's American Indians*. Thunderbird Enterprises.

University Associates (1994). *Highlights of economic impact of Michigan's Indian gaming enterprises*. Lansing, MI: Author.

U.S. General Accounting Office. (1997). *Tax policy: A profile of the Indian gaming industry*. GAO/GGD-97-91. Washington, DC: Author.

Witkins, B.M. & Ritter, B.R. (1994). Will the house win: Does sovereignty rule in Indian casinos? *Great Plains Research, 4*,(2), pp. 305-324.

Yoder, J. (1995). *Federal Indian policy, Secretary of the Interior Bruce Babbitt, and Indian gaming in Arizona*. Tempe, AZ: Arizona State University.

Domestic Violence Among the Navajo: A Legacy of Colonization

Diane McEachern
Marlene Van Winkle
Sue Steiner

SUMMARY. Domestic violence is the leading cause of injuries to women ages 15 to 44. Navajo women have increasingly been plagued by domestic violence and in response, in 1993 the Navajo Nation enacted the Domestic Abuse Prevention Act. Years of colonization have left their mark on members of the Navajo Nation. The Navajo Nation exists within a climate of institutionalized violence, where some of their traditional values of equality and harmony have been broken down. This has led to an increase in family violence. Poverty and a lack of infrastructure and social services exacerbate the problems that Navajo women face when trying to leave violence in their homes. Using information gathered through experience as social workers and ethnographic interviews, this paper explores domestic violence among the Navajo in Northeastern Arizona, with a particular focus on the effects of colonization. *[Article copies available for a fee from The Haworth Document Delivery Service: 1-800-342-9678. E-mail address: getinfo@haworthpressinc.com]*

Diane McEachern, MSW, is affiliated with Arizona State University School of Social Work, PO Box 871802, Tempe, AZ 85287.

Marlene Van Winkle, MSW, is affiliated with Arizona State University School of Social Work, PO Box 871802, Tempe, AZ 85287.

Sue Steiner, PhD, is affiliated with the Arizona State University School of Social Work, Tempe, AZ 85287.

Address correspondence to: Sue Steiner, Arizona State University, School of Social Work, PO Box 871802, Tempe, AZ 85287.

[Haworth co-indexing entry note]: "Domestic Violence Among the Navajo: A Legacy of Colonization." McEachern, Diane, Marlene Van Winkle, and Sue Steiner. Co-published simultaneously in *Journal of Poverty* (The Haworth Press, Inc.) Vol. 2, No. 4, 1998, pp. 31-46; and: *Pressing Issues of Inequality and American Indian Communities* (ed: Elizabeth A. Segal and Keith M. Kilty) The Haworth Press, Inc., 1998, pp. 31-46. Single or multiple copies of this article are available for a fee from The Haworth Document Delivery Service [1-800-342-9678, 9:00 a.m. - 5:00 p.m. (EST). E-mail address: getinfo@haworthpressinc.com].

KEYWORDS. Domestic violence, Native American, American Indian, Navajo, reservation, colonization, rural

INTRODUCTION

The history of colonization has dramatically shaped the experience of many Native People with regards to gender relationships. Among one native community in the Philippines, the Ibaloi, when women are asked what makes a good husband, three areas are mentioned frequently. Women say a good husband is a man who does not drink, does not hit his wife, and is someone who works hard in the field. According to these same women, this set of standards is not "traditional" because there was a time when alcohol consumption and family violence were not part of village life. Alcohol abuse and domestic violence are, to them, part of the "price you have to pay" and " a woman's cross to bear" since the advent of economic and religious colonization. These two statements refer to economic and religious influences that stem from the colonization of the Philippines by both Spain and later the United States.

One forum for the discussion of these and other issues pertinent to Native peoples was the 1987 International Indigenous Peoples Conference sponsored by the Philippine National movement. A Native American delegate from a U.S. reservation commented on his profound experience in one of the remote mountain villages he had visited while in the Philippines. He told the participants that although he was from half way around the world, he felt more at home in the village with tribal Bontoc people than he did in the nearby "border" town near his reservation home in the United States. While he did not speak the Bontoc language, the culture of the people and the manner in which he, as a visitor, was treated overwhelmed him with a sensation of home. The conference contained and generated a rich energy as Indigenous Group delegates from all over the world assessed the "price" they were all paying for the subjugation of their communities to Western, and more specifically, the United States global power.

As do native women in the Philippines, Native American women from a variety of tribes within the United States also bear the brunt of colliding cultures and government colonial policies. This paper presents an exploratory analysis of domestic violence among Navajo Indians of the Southwest United States, with a focus on the Western Navajo Reservation in Arizona. Specific attention is paid to the effects of colonization, the clash between Native American and mainstream American culture, and the effects of living in an isolated rural area.

Information for the paper was gathered through the authors' experiences as social work practitioners working in the area of domestic violence and working with Native Peoples, and through ethnographic research conducted among Navajo men and women in Northeastern Arizona. The authors interviewed community leaders, social service providers, and women who had experienced domestic violence. The latter were contacted through the authors' personal networks and the network of service providers. Interviews were conducted by one of the authors who is a member of the Navajo community. This fluid research methodology is essential, given the cultural-based reluctance to discuss domestic violence that is common among the Navajo, as well as the Navajo community's discomfort with outsiders.

DOMESTIC VIOLENCE

Although women have been beaten within the confines and privacy of their intimate relationships throughout historical record it wasn't until the late 1980s that the Surgeon General of the United States identified domestic violence as the number one public health problem for women. It remains the leading cause of injuries to women ages 15-44. These injuries are more common than muggings, auto accidents, and cancer deaths combined (Dwyer, Smokowski, Bricout, & Wodarski, 1995). The historical context within which battering has developed is that of male domination within and outside the family unit. Throughout most of Western European history, the patriarchal family was directly supported by the laws and practices of the larger society. That historical legacy was brought to the United States and continues to influence the dominant social structure. The patriarchal family predates capitalist society, and so does violence against women within it.

Patriarchal authority is based on male control over woman's productive capacity, and over her person. This control existed before the development of capitalist commodity production. It belonged to a society in which the persons of human beings were owned by others. (Rowbotham, 1973, p. 83)

Pre-capitalist and early capitalist patriarchal authority was based on the father's control of "his" household, which was the focus of daily life and productive activity for everyone. In Western Europe, marriage laws explicitly recognized the family as the domain of the husband, forced women to conform to the man's will, and punished men and women unequally for infractions of marriage vows (Dobash & Dobash, 1979).

In their historical overview of wife beating, Dobash and Dobash (1979) note that, "through the seventeenth, eighteenth, and nineteenth centuries, there was little objection within the community to a man's using force against his wife as long as he did not exceed certain tacit limits" (p. 42). It is this historical reality that is relevant to exploring the development of domestic violence among Native Americans in general, and within the Navajo Nation, more specifically.

DOMESTIC VIOLENCE AMONG NATIVE AMERICANS

Working with Native Americans requires the ability to collapse the past and present into a current reality. Time often takes on a different meaning, with the past feeling like a part of the present. Given this cultural reality, it is impossible to explore a present situation without exploring its historical context. While Native American women come from a diversity of tribal and cultural backgrounds, they share similar experiences and legacies of rapid social change. Much of this change can be directly linked to European colonization, disease decimation from European contact, Christian missionizing, and relocations to "less desirable" geographic areas and/or boarding schools. Although domestic violence is an issue which dates back throughout history among European populations, most scholars of Native American cultures believe that domestic violence is a relatively recent phenomenon which coincides with the advent of colonial rule and the subjugation of Native Americans. As one Navajo woman put it, "A lot of women are having trouble with their husbands. The only model the men have is the macho white man. They try to copy him and Navajo women object" (Shepardson, 1982, p. 101).

There seems to be relatively little information about Native cultures regarding violence against women prior to European contact. What is known is that in most Native American societies men's and women's roles were delineated in such a way that violence against women among their own groups did not seem to be a common and regular practice (Allen, 1986; Neithammer, 1977; Wagner, 1988). For example, among Iroquois women, there was recognition that, ". . . As an Indian woman I was free. I owned my own home, my person, the work of my own hands. I was better as an Indian woman than under white law" (Fletcher, 1888, p. 2). Traditionally, within Navajo culture, women shared equal rights with men, and sometimes enjoyed superior authority and importance. Navajo common law reflected these values through women's property ownership and control, the mother's determinative role in tracing ancestry, and married couples' practice of residing with the wife's family. Some cultures treat women as property, or their culture's law retains vestiges of the notion that women are property. Navajo common law used property and ownership concepts in a different way: "In marriage, . . . a man becomes property of a woman, a woman property of a man" (Zion & Zion, 1993, p. 35). In this way, Navajo common law conceived the reciprocal relations of a man and woman as an interdependent bond. Women's equal status and dignity are reinforced by Navajo literature, which details Navajo women's important work and essential role in society. Their greatest deity, Changing Woman, who is also Mother Earth, symbolizes women's social importance.

In their study of rape and Navajo traditional response to it, Zion and White (1986) could not locate sources which clearly defined early Navajo rape customs. They concluded that rape was relatively absent from early Navajo society. Similarly, they found that the available literature seems to indicate that domestic violence and child abuse were known but were an aberration. Native American scholar Paula Gunn Allen (1986) contends that the crime of domestic violence is caused by economic dislocation, the destruction of traditional institutions, and the introduction of individualism and the individualistic norms of paternalism and patriarchal rule. These new concepts were mandated and forced upon the Native American community in a variety of ways, some of which are described below.

Prior to 1883, marriage practices, divorce, and inheritance were strongholds of women's power within the tribe. Divorce could be enacted by women simply by removing the husband's belongings from the home. Wealth such as animals, the home, and possessions in the family passed through the mother to her daughters. In 1883, the Commissioner of Indian Affairs introduced the Court of Indian Offenses for Indian reservations, where some of the "new" crimes included traditional marriage practices, traditional divorce, and traditional inheritance (Zion & Zion, 1993). The resulting regulations changed the power balance between men and women. The federal government also thought that the best way to "civilize" Indians was to turn them into farmers with exclusive rights to a fixed area of land. The federal government, through the Dawes Act of 1886, required the allotment of Indian lands. These allotments were made to men and not women, further eroding Native American women's power. One of the theories behind the Dawes Act was that individual land ownership would "restore" manhood to Indian men (Deutsch, 1991). The allotment system "was intended to transform Indians who lived under varied kin systems into male-headed, monogamous nuclear families," either ignoring or attacking Indian concepts of family (Scharff, 1991, p. 64).

Another destructive innovation was the adoption of the strong, male leader–"the head man." U.S. government leaders insisted that the Navajos select male leaders (Underhill, 1956). Navajo women had enjoyed a strong role in the public decisions of Navajo clan groups. They lost their ability to participate in decisions made by male leaders given absolute power. Thus, alien law and government destroyed traditional relationships and concentrated power in the hands of male leaders. Without the institutionalized protection of Navajo common law, Navajo women suffered. In this way, non-Indian paternalism and patriarchy were introduced to Navajos. Navajo men learned several Anglo "traditions" including robbing women of economic and political power and wife-beating.

The use of boarding schools is another powerful instituted practice that is repeatedly mentioned when talking with Native Americans about the issues facing them today. Between 1850 and 1950, the federal government practiced widespread systematic removal of Indian children from their families and communities and placed them into state- and church-run boarding schools. This was to become known as "the boarding school era." The boarding school was an important component of the efforts to destroy tribal cultures. For many people these schools were a traumatic experience that included physical, sexual and emotional abuse. The Federal government implemented coordinated efforts to eradicate each tribe's religion, identity, language, and social organization. The effects of these destructive efforts still reverberate at many levels including the family. Away from their families, prohibited from speaking their languages and practicing their traditions, generations of Indian children grew up in institutions that widely used corporal punishment as a means of "socialization" (Brown, 1971). The Federal government's decision to remove native children from their communities and place then in church-run boarding schools is described by Native American writer Eileen Hudson (1995) as:

> . . . a heinous act designed to destroy the emotional and spiritual heart of those communities. This process tore away at the notions of tribal continuity, inheritance, native intellectual knowledge, and sustainable infrastructures for native society. It left a people stunned from the seemingly silent and invisible atrocities created when a nation's future is sequestered away. (p. 76)

Interviews conducted by the authors often included mention of the boarding schools. One Navajo man, a Traditional Counselor, was asked to give his view of domestic violence. He began recounting an incident that happened to him when he was going to a boarding school. He spoke of the harsh treatment he and other children received. He told of priests who sexually abused boys and how cruel some of the teachers were. He then went further back in history and talked about why hogans are constructed in the shape they are. He said that a hogan represents the center of the family and community and it is round to replicate the body of a pregnant woman. The logs used in construction represent her hands clasped around her belly. He explained that "home is wherever woman is." At first we tried to ask about domestic violence in other ways to try and get him to say something about the present situation but each time he would refer back to boarding school times. To this man, domestic violence was not defined merely in terms of abuse occurring within the home, but more broadly as that which was done to Native Americans through the use of boarding schools.

DOMESTIC VIOLENCE AMONG THE NAVAJO

The Navajo Nation is the largest and most populous American Indian Nation with over 250,000 members. Spanning Arizona, New Mexico and Utah, the Navajo Nation encompasses 17.5 million acres–and is larger than the states of Connecticut, Delaware, Maryland, Massachusetts and Rhode Island combined. The 1990 Census reports that the percentage of Navajos living below the poverty level was approximately 56 percent as compared to approximately 13 percent for the United States. The average annual per capita income of the Navajo people was $4,106 compared to the U.S. average of $19,082 in 1990. Navajo unemployment ranges from 36 percent to over 50 percent seasonally. Navajo Nation President Albert A. Hale (1996) further describes conditions on the Reservation:

> . . . many of these conditions can be attributed to a lack of infrastructure which itself is directly related to the failure of the Federal government to live up to its trust and treaty responsibilities. For example, the Navajo reservation has 2,000 miles of paved roads while West Virginia, which is roughly equivalent in size, has over 18,000 miles. Similarly, the vast majority of Navajo homes lack electricity, running water and telephones, or all of the above. (p. 4)

Domestic violence is a growing problem on the Navajo reservation, and it is particularly difficult in Western Navajo. Western

Navajo has a varied topography, generally mountainous with deep canyon lands. For every dirt road there is a corresponding footpath and many families live miles from other families. The largest town in the area is Tuba City with a population of 8,000. Although Western Navajo has the second highest population and covers one-third of the total Reservation land area, it has the fewest services for women and children victims of domestic violence. Without a phone, money, and transportation, and with miles between houses, a Navajo woman faces a formidable challenge in attempting to leave a violent partner. People on the reservation live in geographically rural areas with long distances between services. This further complicates the issue of family violence. Rural populations are generally not large enough to support specialized services, and transportation is a perennial problem. There is a high lack of awareness of services, or knowledge as to whether a battered woman's shelter could, in fact, provide emergency transport. There is no phone service to many households. Specific to reservation life, if a woman wants to leave her abusive partner, she may need to leave the reservation. This means leaving her family network. Often, she will not be able to find work in the nearby border towns and returning to the reservation and the perpetrator becomes the lesser of two evils, especially when her children are involved.

Perpetrators of domestic violence have a sense of how to maintain control over their victims. They know that phones, money and transportation can be vital links to a woman's ability to escape to safety. Many of the conditions that exist within the Navajo Nation in general, and in the Western Navajo more specifically, exacerbate the problem of domestic violence, and limit a woman's opportunities to leave violent situations. The following anecdotes, with details changed to preserve anonymity, are representative of stories heard often from women on the reservation, and express many of the dilemmas a Navajo woman faces:

> May, a Navajo woman, dropped her husband off at the trading post on the Navajo Reservation so he could unload hay. As she drove off she became stuck in mud. As a result, she was late in returning to pick up her husband. In a rage, he hit her repeatedly in front of the children while they were in the trading post parking lot. During the attack, the three young children

screamed for him to stop. Badly beaten, with a serious eye injury, the woman fled and walked for hours in the snow until she came to a home where she was allowed to stay the night. There was no telephone, and with the severe shortage of Navajo police she might not have gotten assistance from them. The next day, she again set off on foot until she came to another house where the family had a car and gas and was able to drive her 50 miles to the hospital so she could have her eye treated.

A Navajo woman was severely beaten by her husband in her home. Her children ran from the house to get help from relatives about a half mile down the road. A relative notified police officers and requested an ambulance. The ambulance arrived first, but the paramedics found that the road to the home was too muddy for the ambulance to get through. The paramedics began to walk through the mud to the house, and were eventually picked up by police officers whose vehicle was able to make it through the mud. The woman was severely hurt, and was taken from her home by the paramedics in the police vehicle, which became stuck in the mud while leaving the house. The vehicle was eventually freed from the mud, and the woman taken to a hospital. Unfortunately, the length of time that it took the police and paramedics to arrive allowed the husband to flee, and the delays meant that a great deal of time passed before the woman was able to get medical attention.

Sometime in 1991, Sara was beaten by her husband, Ned. They are Navajo and live with their two toddlers and baby on the Navajo Reservation. Ned had been drinking when he began hitting and screaming at Sara. Ned kept a gun in the house and had threatened to kill Sara a number of times. She decided to take the beating and hope that he would soon pass out so she could escape with the children. They did not own a phone, there was no cash in the house, and the car was not running.

Ned soon passed out and Sara, experiencing back pain, extensive bruises and a swollen eye, gathered her children and left the house. She carried the baby while the two toddlers walked beside her. It was summer and as the heat began pressing on the day, Sara and the children walked 2 miles on a dirt path to a main road which was also unpaved. She then hitched a ride 10 miles to the Trading Post, a small store located in most Chapter House areas. No one was around so she walked a mile to the Chapter House office building. There was a phone there but, as is common, it was broken. As luck would have it, a police officer drove by and Sara flagged him down. It was rare good fortune because there are only 5 police officers patrolling the 4,100 square mile area. The officer drove her and her exhausted children 50 miles to a relay point. Another police officer picked her up and took her to the nearest shelter which was 100 miles away. The shelter was full. They found another shelter in a nearby town outside the reservation with space. By that time it was about 8 o'clock at night. Sara and the children eventually returned to Ned.

CONTRADICTIONS WITHIN LAW ENFORCEMENT

"Equality of rights under the law shall not be denied or abridged by the Navajo Nation on account of sex . . . " so reads the Navajo Nation Bill of Rights. What U.S. women could not get passed before the national government, Navajo women were accorded outright. Yet due to the various conditions outlined previously, it is difficult for law enforcement to be of much assistance to women who are being battered in their homes.

The small town of Kayenta, in Western Navajo, has just five officers patrolling 4,100 square miles. The officers are responsible for 15,270 people. Police in this endless horizon of red rock formations and valleys aren't unlike those in other rural, poor districts around the nation. For Navajo officers, however, the task is compounded by the reservation's horrifying host of social ills: unemployment, alcoholism, suicide and murder rates multiple times the national average. It is particularly challenging for police in this area. In the past nine years, three officers were murdered on the job, one committed suicide and another was jailed for killing his wife (Boorstein, 1997). Navajo police chief Leonard Butler noted the changes for police, saying, "When I started in 1971, a lot of our time was taken up with livestock being shot or windmill disputes.

Now, in one week I've got two fatal accidents, one suicide and five people killed. There are times when you don't want to go to work anymore."

Navajo officers mirror their community. Alcohol and drug abuse, divorce, domestic violence or suicide seem to touch nearly every life. Often they blame the victim in domestic violence disputes, saying she must have done something to bring on the abuse. In this way they conform to the attitude of many law officers in the U.S. For all of these reasons, some Navajo women are concerned that in domestic violence situations, help from law enforcement officers may not be readily available.

DIRECTIONS FOR INTERVENTION

In July 1993, the Navajo Nation enacted the Domestic Abuse Prevention Act. This Act states that domestic violence is a crime, specifies that protection is to be provided for all populations, outlines services for victims, and specifies penalties for perpetrators.

The Resolution of the Navajo Nation Council (CJY-52-93) accompanying the Act states:

1. Domestic violence is occurring on the Navajo Nation in epidemic proportions. Many Navajo persons are beaten, harassed, threatened or otherwise subjected to abuse within the domestic setting; and
2. Domestic violence has a lasting detrimental effect on the individuals who directly experience the abuse and on their children, who carry memories of violence with them into their adult lives and may themselves become violent and abusive.

This legislation demonstrates the Navajo Nation's commitment to addressing the issue of domestic violence, and provides a strong foundation on which interventive efforts can be built. Discussions with Navajo women suggest a possible direction for intervention which deserves further attention. Within many Native cultures when a breakup happened as a result of abuse, the woman who left was viewed as honorable for having the respect and dignity to leave a destructive relationship behind. She did not have to fear retaliation or terrorism. The husband recognized her right to make her own choices and if he could not respect this, the Tribe intervened to insure her safety and teach him proper behavior (Balzer et al. 1993). Navajo women with whom we spoke no longer feel that they would be respected in that way. One woman described her deep shame and embarrassment when her partner abused her. She was extremely afraid of her partner and tried to keep the problems hidden for as long as she could until he almost killed her.

There are women who have been victims and have been able to leave their abusers and get help. One of those women who was interviewed on the reservation said that she saw a connection between women battering and subjugation in other forms. She described how these acts of violence have the same dynamics as those of the invasion of one country by another, the master over slave, the colonization of native people, and Western men's subjugation of women. This suggests that an interventive approach that might prove effective with Navajo women could be built on the work of Brazilian educator Paulo Freire (1970). Freire writes about peasants, and how they can use liberating education to overcome oppression and transform their situations. The descriptions of the oppressed peasants fit victims of domestic violence quite well. He describes the peasants as people who feel that they do not know things, that they do not know how to change things, that distrust themselves, and that are very self-deprecating. "So often do they hear that they are good for nothing, know nothing and are incapable of learning anything–that they are sick, lazy, and unproductive–that in the end they become convinced of their own unfitness" (p. 45). This leaves them believing that they do not know how and that they are unable to change their current situations.

Freire stresses that to overcome oppression and to leave oppressive situations, reflection is essential. We must reflect on our situation, before we can act to change it. He points out the importance of gaining a critical awareness of oppression through dialogue and what he calls "liberating education." Liberating education means not talking at people, not explaining to people, but dialoguing with them. It means helping them to develop a critical consciousness by having conversations with others who are in a similar situation, or have been in a similar situation. This can be done through dialogue groups, where women can come together to explore their lives, and to make connections between their situations and the bigger picture. To do this we must first trust that these women are capable of looking critically at their lives, and capable of reason and reflection. We must also trust that they have the answers and must find them through conversation and struggle with others. This means abandoning our efforts to tell Navajo women in battering situations what they must do, and instead supporting them in their development of a critical consciousness gained through dialogue.

Freire's work may also suggest a direction to take with Navajo batterers. Freire stresses that those who are oppressed emulate their oppressor, and become emotionally dependent. This leads them to take out their frustrations on others who are oppressed around them.

> The peasant is a dependent. He can't say what he wants. Before he discovers his dependence, he suffers. He lets off steam at home, where he shouts at his children, beats them, and despairs. He complains about his wife and thinks everything is dreadful. He doesn't let off steam with the boss because he thinks the boss is a superior being. Lots of times, the peasant gives vent to his sorrows by drinking. (Freire, 1970, p. 47)

Some of the violence of Navajo men toward their female partners may be a result of their own oppression. These men can be helped to understand how the various forms of oppression are related, and how their oppression by the dominant society is resulting in their taking their frustration out at home. Dialogue groups with the male batterers, that focus on consciousness raising and their experience as Native American men in an Anglo-dominated society, can help them better understand themselves and their actions. Dialogue groups could also help them develop more appropriate options for handling their anger and frustration.

Interventions based on Freire's work on liberating education are culturally relevant for the Navajo given the Navajo's experience of colonization and oppression. Freire's model was developed with South American peasants, many of whom, like the Navajo, were living in rural, generally isolated areas. They had also experienced years of colonization and oppression, and extreme poverty. Use of Freire's model also seems appropriate given that it is an intervention that does not require outsiders to come in and try to "fix" the problem for those living on the reservation, as has been tried by Anglos for many years.

Years of colonization have left their mark on members of the Navajo Nation. The Navajo Nation exists within a climate of institutionalized violence, where some of their traditional values of equality and harmony have been broken down. This has led to an increase in family violence. Poverty and a lack of infrastructure and social services exacerbate the problems that Navajo women face when trying to leave violence in their homes. Future research must continue to document the prevalence and severity of the problem of domestic violence on the Navajo reservation, and culturally relevant interventions must be developed and evaluated.

REFERENCES

Allen, Paula Gunn. (1986). *The Sacred Hoop: Recovering the Feminine in American Indian Traditions*. Boston: Beacon Press.

Balzer, R., James, G., LaPrarie, L., & Olson, T. (1993). *Mending to Sacred Circle: Coming Back to Where we Began*. Duluth, MN.

Boorstein, M. (1997, February 24). Lonely, deadly police work. *Arizona Republic*, p. 1.

Brown, D. (1971). *Bury My Heart at Wounded Knee*. New York: Holt, Reinhart, & Winston.

Deutsch, S. (1991). Coming together, coming apart–Women's history and the west. *Montana Magazine of Western History, 41*, 58-60.

Dobash, E. & Dobash, R. (1979). *Violence Against Wives: A Case against the Patriarchy*. New York: The Free Press.

Dwyer, D., Smokowski, P., Bricout, J., & Wodarski, J. (1995). Domestic violence research: Theoretical and practical implications for social work. *Clinical Social Work Journal, 23*, 185-198.

Fletcher, Alice. (1888). *Report of the International Council of Women*. Washington DC: Darby Printer.

Freire, P. (1970). *Pedagogy of the Oppressed*. New York: Continuum Publishing Co.

Hale, A. (1996). The Navajo Nation Report. Office of the President and Vice President, The Navajo Nation.

Hudson, E. (1995). *Mending to Sacred Circle: Coming Back to Where we Began*. Duluth, MN.

Neithammer, C. (1977). *Daughters of the Earth: The Lives and Legends of American Indian Women*. New York: Macmillan.

Rowbotham, S. (1973). *Women and Revolution*. London: Routledge & Kegan.

Scharff, M. (1991). Gender and Western History: Is anybody home on the range? *Montana Magazine of West History, 41*, 62-65.

Shepardson, M. (1982). The Status of Navajo Women. *American Indian Quarterly*, 6.

Underhill, R. (1956). *Navajos*. Norman, OK: University of Oklahoma Press.

Wagner, S. (1988). The Root of Oppression is the Loss of Memory: The Iroquois and the Early Feminist Vision. Paper delivered at the 1988 Champlian Valley Historical Symposium. Plattsburgh, New York.

Zion, J. & White, M. (1986). The Use of Navajo Custom in Dealing with Rape. In Indian Health Service (ed.) *Final Report: A Case Study of Family Violence in Four Native American Communities*. Washington, DC: Department of Health and Human Services.

Zion, J. & Zion, E. (1993). Hozho's Sokee'–Stay Together Nicely: Domestic violence under Navajo common law. *Arizona State Law Journal*, 25.

The Health of Alaska Native Women: Significant Problems, Emerging Solutions

Donna E. Hurdle

SUMMARY. Native American women living in Alaska have a number of health problems with higher incidence and mortality rates than other women in the United States. These include certain cancers (cervical, lung), sexually transmitted diseases (chlamydia, human papilomavirus), and use of alcohol and tobacco. These health concerns are exacerbated by restricted access to medical services, lack of culturally sensitive health promotion efforts by health providers, and Native women's limited use of preventive health behaviors. Suggestions for health promotion with this population include framing health promotion in a holistic manner that includes Native values and spirituality, use of cultural symbols (such as the talking stick), and cultural teaching traditions (talking circle, story-telling). *[Article copies available for a fee from The Haworth Document Delivery Service: 1-800-342-9678. E-mail address: getinfo@haworthpressinc.com]*

KEYWORDS. Culturally sensitive health promotion, Alaska Native, women's health

Until recent years, the health of American women was virtually ignored by government funding and medical researchers, who focused their attention on diseases predominantly affecting men, and

Donna E. Hurdle, PhD, is Assistant Professor, Arizona State University School of Social Work, PO Box 871802, Tempe, AZ 85287-1802.

[Haworth co-indexing entry note]: "The Health of Alaska Native Women: Significant Problems, Emerging Solutions." Hurdle, Donna E. Co-published simultaneously in *Journal of Poverty* (The Haworth Press, Inc.) Vol. 2, No. 4, 1998, pp. 47-61; and: *Pressing Issues of Inequality and American Indian Communities* (ed: Elizabeth A. Segal and Keith M. Kilty) The Haworth Press, Inc., 1998, pp. 47-61. Single or multiple copies of this article are available for a fee from The Haworth Document Delivery Service [1-800-342-9678, 9:00 a.m. - 5:00 p.m. (EST). E-mail address: getinfo@haworthpressinc.com].

used male subjects almost exclusively in drug testing (Healy, 1991a, 1991b). This situation resulted in inadequate medical treatment for women, particularly in the area of heart disease, and a lack of progress in determining the causation of and treatments for various women's diseases (Council on Ethical and Judicial Affairs, American Medical Association, 1991). Scientific journals from a variety of fields (medicine, public health, nursing, and social work) have deplored this situation and called for adequate funding of research on women's health and the full participation of female subjects in all clinical trials (Clancy & Massion, 1992; Healy, 1991a, 1991b; Olson, 1994). The social work profession has also identified women's health as a priority for research, including the specific health problems of women of color, and the development of new service delivery models that recognize the unique experiences of women and build on their strengths (National Committee on Women's Issues, 1996).

Given this historical lack of research attention to women's health, the specific health concerns of women of color have been virtually ignored. Of all ethnic groups, the health and well-being of American Indian and Alaska Native women are substandard in comparison to other women in the United States (Joe, 1996). Native American women have health problems that are more pervasive and life threatening than majority group women or other women of color, and also differ from Native American males (Lutz, 1997). While health issues vary to some degree between tribal groups and regions, there are certain diseases, such as cervical cancer, that disproportionately affect Native women in many different areas of the country. Other such diseases are lung, gallbladder, kidney, and stomach cancer, sexually transmitted diseases (such as chlamydia), and alcohol-related diseases, including fetal alcohol syndrome in children (Nutting et al., 1993). Complicating these health problems are issues of socioeconomic status, including a high percentage of Native women living in poverty, lack of formal education, limited employment, and limited access to health care when living on reservations or in communities located in rural areas without public transportation (Joe, 1996). As a result of all these factors, American Indian women have poorer health status than either Caucasian or other minority populations on a number of indicators (Joe, 1996; Nutting et al., 1993).

For many health problems, prevention or early detection practices exist, but may not be available or are not being utilized by Native American women. Preventive health practices, such as Pap tests, mammography, and screening for sexually transmitted disease, are not being performed, despite the availability of subsidized health care through the Indian Health Service. In fact, the Indian Health Service (part of the Public Health Service) does not provide services to all Native Americans in the United States, and served only 63% of this population in 1993 (Lutz, 1997). The limited use of preventive health practices by Native women can be explained by the lack of culturally appropriate health promotion efforts, lack of access to care in remote areas, and value differences between Native Americans and majority health care providers (Joe, 1996; Michielutte, Sharp, Dignan, & Blinson, 1994). Disease prevention efforts with indigenous populations must integrate the values and health practices of the culture in order to be effective (Han et al., 1994).

The health concerns of Native women in Alaska are unique in a number of ways. Their incidence and mortality rates for certain diseases are higher than those of Native American women living in other parts of the country, other Alaskan women, or all women in the United States. These diseases include cancers of the salivary gland, nasopharynx, colorectal, liver, pancreas, lung, and kidney (Nutting et al., 1993). Higher rates of sexually transmitted disease, including gonorrhea and chlamydia, have also been found for Alaska Native women (Davidson et al., 1994). The prevalence of current smoking is 50% in this group of women, in addition to the use of smokeless tobacco, which contributes to their five-fold increase in lung cancer between 1969-88 (Lanier et al., 1994).

Alaska Native women are the most high-risk group of women in the country for some cancers, reproductive health problems, and detrimental lifestyle practices including smoking and excessive use of alcohol (Lanier, Bulkow, & Ireland, 1989). The unique geography in which they live, the difficulties in providing health care in such an environment, and limited culturally appropriate health promotion efforts all negatively impact the health of Alaska Native women. To fully understand the health issues of Alaska Native women, one must first be aware of the geographical, political, and cultural context of their lives.

ALASKA NATIVE PEOPLES

Alaska is the largest state in the union, encompassing about one-fifth of the total land mass of the contiguous United States (Shumacher, Lanier, & Owen, 1997). Due to its size, there are large variations in the topography and climate from one part of the state to the other. This geographical context strongly influences the lifestyles and cultural patterns of Alaska's Native peoples. Alaska is largely composed of small communities, which are located at some distance from others. Half of the state's population of approximately 550,000 lives in Anchorage, which is the largest city in the state, while others live in small towns and native villages. There is no road system to 80% of Alaska's rural, predominantly native communities. Many villages are accessible only by air or water, which makes access a significant challenge, particularly during winter months. This geography has a significant impact on the health delivery system in Alaska, making access to care problematic in many parts of the state.

The indigenous peoples of Alaska, collectively designated "Alaska Natives," are composed of different tribal groups with distinctive language, heritage, and cultural patterns. They have lived historically in different parts of the state, the topography of which influenced their subsistence patterns. The state's population is 16% Alaska Native, a significantly larger indigenous population than the United States as a whole (.8%), with a total Native population of 86,252 in 1990 (Schumacher et al., 1997). Approximately 60% of all Native peoples live in communities historically inhabited by their ancestors, which range from 20 to 5,000 people (Stillwater, Echavarria, & Lanier, 1995).

The Native peoples of Alaska include Eskimos, Indians, and Aleuts. Within these three major ethnic groups, multiple linguistic and cultural subgroups can be identified including four Eskimo groups (Sugpiaq, Central and Siberian Yupik, and Inupiaq), four Indian groups (Athabascan, Tlingit, Tsimpsian, and Haida) and Aleuts (Stillwater et al., 1995). Just over half of the Native population is Eskimo, one-sixth are Aleut, and the rest are Indian (Schumacher et al., 1997).

Historically, Alaska Natives did not have treaties with the federal government or tribal status, with the exception of one reservation (Metakatla). The Alaska Native Claims Settlement Act was passed by Congress in 1971 to compensate Alaska Natives for the loss of their traditional lands in order to develop the oil reserves on the north coast of Alaska (Kizzia, 1997). This act established land-owning native corporations with native shareholders, granting them a total of $962 million dollars. Regional native organizations of different ethnic heritage were created in different parts of the state; the organizations are for-profit entities engaged in business development, which also have a non-profit arm to provide health and social service functions. Health services have been integrated with the Indian Health Service in many locations, and consist of regionally based hospitals, itinerant services of various types, and village-based health aides (paraprofessionals).

After passage of the Native Claims Settlement Act, the federal government determined that tribal status had been extinguished with the creation of the new native corporations. This controversial decision was strongly contested by Native groups. Eventually, officials of the Clinton administration in the Bureau of Indian Affairs reversed this decision, and designated 226 Alaska native villages as tribes in 1993 (Kizzia, 1997). However, Alaska was still not considered "Indian country," a legal term indicating native rights to land, mineral resources, and self-governance, including taxation. In November 1996, the Federal 9th Circuit Court ruled that Indian country does exist in Alaska, specifically in the village of Venetie (Hunter, 1997). This decision is currently on appeal to the U.S. Supreme Court, with a decision expected at the end of the 1998 session. The outcome of the Supreme Court decision will have a great influence on the future of sovereignty and self-governance for Alaska Natives. This decision may also influence the provision of health care to Alaska Natives, as the roles of native organizations and tribes may change, and different relationships with the Indian Health Service or the state health department may develop.

Within the political context of an on-going struggle for self-determination, Alaska Natives are struggling to integrate their cultural heritage with the demands of 20th century America. Over half of the population of Alaska Natives lives in more than 200 isolated villages. For these individuals, tribal councils largely determine the context of village life, and cultural traditions strongly influence family functioning and community activities. However, television, travel, and village-based schools have brought western values into the villages, which are particularly appealing to the young. The other half of the Alaska Native population lives in urban situations, often in poverty. The tension between traditional and modern values and lifestyles results in many psychological and health problems, including high rates of alcohol use, depression and suicide (Alaska Federation of Natives, 1995). Access to health care is also a significant problem for many, as a paraprofessional health aide is the only medical provider in most Native villages. These various factors combine to reduce the life expectancy of Alaska Natives by seven years in comparison to other Alaskan residents. At almost every age, Alaska Natives are at greater risk of death than are non-Natives; the leading causes of death among Natives are unintentional injuries, cancer, and heart disease (Schumacher et al., 1997). The health issues of Native women are different than those of males or children, and in many ways are more severe.

HEALTH PROBLEMS OF ALASKA NATIVE WOMEN

Alaska Native women have the highest mortality rate of women of any ethnic group in the United States (Miller et al., 1996). They also have the highest cancer mortality rates of all U.S. women, largely because of high smoking rates (Schumacher et al., 1997). Cancer is the leading cause of death of Alaska Native women, and breast cancer is the most commonly diagnosed cancer among Alaska Native women, followed by lung cancer, and cervical cancer (Davidson et al., 1994; Lanier, 1996; Schumacher, Lanier, & Owen, 1997; Stillwater et al., 1995). These diseases result in the loss of many years of life for Alaska Native women.

Lung cancer is the leading cause of cancer death in both the United States and the state of Alaska, where the rate is somewhat higher; Alaska native people have a higher mortality rate from lung cancer than non-natives in Alaska (Shumacher, Landen et al., 1997). The incidence of lung cancer in Alaska Natives now exceeds the U.S. rate, after many years at lower levels; the prevalence of smoking in Alaska Natives is nearly double the national average (Lanier, 1996). The Alaska mortality rate for breast cancer is slightly less than the rate for the rest of the country; however, Alaska Native women living in urban areas have twice the mortality rate from breast cancer as do Native women living in rural areas (Schumacher, Landen et al., 1997).

Alaska Native women have higher cervical cancer mortality rates than the overall Alaskan population (Schumacher, Lanier, & Owen, 1997). They also have the highest cervical cancer incidence rate of any racial group in the United States; their cancer rate is anywhere from three to five times higher than that for white females and 40% greater than that of other American Indian women (Davidson et al., 1994; Provost, 1996). Most alarming is the increasing incidence of cervical cancer in Alaska Natives, at a time when it is declining for other ethnic groups (Davidson et al., 1994).

In addition to cancer, sexually transmitted disease (gonorrhea, chlamydia, and others) has historically had a three to five times higher prevalence in Alaska natives in comparison to non-natives (Davidson et al., 1994). Evidence exists to implicate sexually trans-mitted disease (specifically human papilomavirus [HPV]) in the causation of cervical cancer, as well as smoking, multiple sex part-ners, multiple pregnancies, early age at first intercourse, and early age at first pregnancy (Hislop et al., 1994; Davidson et al., 1994).

Alaska Native women have higher morbidity and mortality than other Alaskan women and in some cases, more than other women in the United States. With the lack of research attention to women's health nationally, these women are doubly disadvantaged by being female and of ethnic origin. Disease prevention and health promo-tion efforts that are culturally sensitive and tailored to specific tribal groups are needed to reduce the high incidence of death and disease among Alaska Native women.

CULTURALLY SENSITIVE HEALTH PROMOTION PROGRAMS

In recent years, there have been efforts in many parts of the country to develop health promotion programs tailored to the needs of specific ethnic groups. Typically, these programs are focused on the prevention of one or two diseases, such as alcoholism, or breast and cervical cancer. The National Cancer Institute has funded several projects to reduce cancer mortality from breast, cervical and lung cancers among Native American populations (Burhansstipanov, 1993). These include avoidable mortality and primary prevention projects with Native Americans in Alaska, Hawaii, North Carolina, Minnesota, Oregon, California and other states. Several of these programs have developed valuable information about the qualities of effective health promotion with Native American tribal groups.

The North Carolina Project, in an effort to develop a culturally sensitive health promotion program, incorporated Native American beliefs and values into the design of their cervical cancer prevention program (Michielutte et al., 1994). Their research indicated that many beliefs and values of Native Americans are antithetical to health prevention efforts. These include an emphasis on living in the present, a belief that health represents a balance between the individual and nature, a fatalistic attitude toward disease, and a reluctance to dwell on illness or negative events (Michielutte et al., 1994). These values, as well as the use of a community-based approach, were instrumental in designing a cervical cancer education and screening project for the Cherokee and Lumbee Indians of North Carolina (Dignan et al., 1993).

Before initiating the project, the tribal councils of the target groups were asked to approve the project, in order to develop local ownership of the effort (Michielutte et al., 1994). After this occurred, and the grant was received, other community leaders and members were involved in individual interviews and focus groups. The prototype cervical cancer education program was then presented to community members for feedback. The project was designed to use lay educators, who were American Indian women from the target communities, in a one-to-one approach of providing education to community women in their homes. Results of the project indicate that this approach was successful in both increasing the knowledge of American Indian women about cervical cancer, and promoting the use of Pap smears to detect cervical cancer (Dignan et al., 1996).

The importance of cultural values in decisions about health be-haviors was also found in a study with the Cheyenne River Sioux (Han et al., 1994). This study found that women with healthier behavior patterns, using a standardized Center for Disease Control instrument, scored higher on cultural factors indicating a more traditional Lakota lifestyle, such as fluency in the Lakota language, a greater degree of Indian blood, and adherence to a traditional lifestyle. In this study, traditional beliefs and limited acculturation into mainstream America were found to be associated with healthy lifestyles. Thus, the importance of framing health promotion efforts in the context of specific tribal cultures, and building on current healthy lifestyles, is underscored.

In addition to cultural values, Native American beliefs and their understanding of particular diseases should be incorporated into the design of health promotion programs. Strickland and her colleagues (1996) studied the meaning of the Pap test and cervical cancer screening to Yakama women in Washington State, in preparation for designing a cervical cancer screening intervention. She found that Yakama women associated the Pap test with being sexually active and, therefore, found it unnecessary once they were past their reproductive years. During their child-bearing years, they had Pap tests in the family planning clinic and associated them with staying healthy, not preventing cancer. Mid-life and elder women avoided going to the doctor due to dissatisfaction with prior medical experi-ences and communication with health care providers. They also felt that Western medicine was not responsive to the Indian view of health as holistic and community based. Strickland and her col-leagues suggest that health promotion programs use respected el-ders to provide health-related teaching in a manner consistent with native traditions of story-telling and talking circles. Messages should be focused on staying healthy, rather than preventing disease or death, and be framed in terms of contributing to the community by staying well. Some of this information is consistent with the cultural values identified in the North Carolina Study (Michielutte et al., 1994).

While a number of community-based health promotion programs for minority communities have been developed in the past few years, most emphasize access to care, one-stop medical services, and case management follow-up (Black, Schweitzer, & Dezelsky, 1993). While these approaches may be useful for many, most of these studies actually serve a small percentage of minority communities. In contrast, health promotion that emphasizes specific cultural values and indigenous views of disease has a far greater potential for impacting the health decisions and behaviors of ethnic communities.

HEALTH PROMOTION PROGRAMS
FOR ALASKA NATIVE WOMEN

In Alaska, a program to prevent cervical cancer is being provided by the Alaska Area Native Health Service (an Indian Health Service Program) in collaboration with a Native organization serving natives in a remote area, the Aleutian/Pribiloff Islands Association (Burhansstipanov, 1993). One of the NCI funded programs, the Alaska Native Women's Health Project, examined the medical records of an urban and rural sample of 528 Alaska Native women to ascertain their screening history, risk factors, and knowledge about cervical cancer. It was found that most women were not aware of the importance of Pap tests, and less than half could identify its purpose (Stillwater et al., 1995). The service delivery component of this project provides a women's health clinic at the Alaska Native Medical Center (an Indian Health Service hospital located in Anchorage) that has evening hours, female providers, and comprehensive education and health services. This is an example of specialized medical services for Alaska Native women that needs to be provided on an on-going basis. This approach responds to needs for confidentiality and staffing by female providers identified by other northwest Native women (Strickland et al., 1996).

The Alaska Women's Health Project also determined that there was a lack of culturally appropriate health education materials for Alaska Native women. To meet this need, a culturally sensitive cervical cancer prevention video was developed and pilot tested (Stillwater et al., 1995). It was found to increase the knowledge level of Native women about cervical cancer, and to be well received due to its use of Native women as role models. The project also developed a pamphlet on breast cancer and screening methods that used paintings of Native women by a local Alaskan artist (Alaska Native Women's Wellness Project, 1996). Other cancer prevention efforts for Alaska Native women have included a breast cancer prevention videotape (Hurdle & Tellman, 1994), which demonstrated breast self-examination and was sent to all paraprofessional health aides in native villages. A community-based health promotion guide was also developed for local Alaskan communities, with instructions on how to implement breast cancer education programs.

While these methods may be useful, they are still Western-oriented health promotion efforts, and may not be as ideal as an approach that reflects the cultural traditions of particular Alaska Native tribal groups, and is based on their values and health beliefs.

New Directions for Health Promotion for Alaska Native Women

To tailor health promotion programs to particular Alaska Native tribes, investigation into their values and attitudes toward health and disease would be most helpful. However, until this is available, information about values and health gathered from other northwest Native women could be utilized. Framing health messages in a holistic manner, emphasizing the importance of women's health to the community, using elders as providers of the intervention, and incorporating cultural traditions into health messages have been found to be important to Native women in Washington state (Strickland et al., 1996). It is particularly important to move away from programs focusing on the prevention of one disease. Native Americans do not view health in a partialized manner, as do the American medical establishment and most health professionals. Rather, health is a physical, emotional and spiritual process that is grounded in the community and the natural environment.

Health professionals must learn to look at illness in the context of spirituality, as this is the basis for traditional healing by curanderos and medicine men and women (Molina, 1997). To be consonant with this view, programs should involve respected tribal spiritual leaders or healers (medicine men or women, or ministers of the Native American church) in some manner. These important individuals could be involved in the delivery of educational programs, or in suggesting attendance to tribal members. To incorporate the native connection to the environment in health promotion, sessions could be held in physical environments that have symbolic value (the church, or outside near sacred mountains). Use of a medicine wheel or other traditional symbols would set the context for an integrated and holistic approach, in which personal health of mind, body, and spirit is related to community health and well-being. Health messages should incorporate this holistic view by connecting physical health to psychological health, with both as a way of contributing to the community.

Alaska Native tradition teaches children values and how to live through stories told by elders, who are role models (John, 1997). Adapting this approach to health promotion, through the use of talking circles and/or story knives, would enhance the cultural relevance of the presentation. Using elders to present health-related information would increase its impact due to the respected position of these individuals in the tribe, and their traditional role as providers of knowledge to the next generation (John, 1997).

Reaching Alaska Native women in rural villages is of vital importance, as these women have the most limited access to medical care. Their resources for health information are also the most limited, as the village health aide (a paraprofessional) is their primary provider. The state-run rural television network could be instrumental in meeting this need by airing video programs specifically developed for these rural Native women. As these women are generally more traditional than women who are living in urban settings, incorporating native values into health messages will be crucial for the video program to be successful.

CONCLUSION

Alaska Native women have a higher risk of morbidity and mortality from certain cancers (cervix, nasopharyngeal, gallbladder, stomach, liver, lung) than all other women in the United States (Lanier, 1993). They are also at high risk for sexually transmitted disease, and health problems secondary to smoking and use of alcohol (Davidson et al., 1994; Lanier, 1996). Several new initiatives have been developed to provide disease prevention efforts to this population; however, they are using typical western health promotion methods, which have had limited success with other native groups (Dignan et al., 1993). Health promotion programs provided to American Indians in other states indicate that cultural sensitivity is a key factor in the effectiveness of health promotion programs (Strickland et al., 1996; Michielutte et al., 1994). Innovative health promotion programs need to be developed for Alaska Native women that reflect their cultural traditions, view health in the context of the community, and are holistic rather than focused on a particular disease process.

REFERENCES

Alaska Native Women's Wellness Project. (1996). Breast cancer screening: A healthy habit for life. (Available from Southcentral Foundation, 670 Fireweed Lane, Anchorage, AK 99504.)

Alaska Federation of Natives. (1995). Ten Year Report: Executive Summary.

Black, B.L., Schweitzer, R., & Dezelsky, T. (1993). Report on the American Cancer Society workshop on community cancer detection, education, and prevention demonstration project for underserved populations. *CA-A Cancer Journal for Clinicians, 43,* 226-233.

Burhansstipanov, L. (1993). National Cancer Institute's Native American cancer research projects. *Alaska Medicine, 35,* 248-55.

Clancy, C.M., & Massion, C.T. (1992). American women's health care: A patchwork quilt with gaps. *Journal of the American Medical Association, 268,* 1918-20.

Council on Ethical and Judicial Affairs, American Medical Association. (1991). Gender disparities in clinical decision making. *Journal of the American Medical Association, 266,* 559-562.

Davidson, M., Schnitzer, P.G., Bulkow, L.R., Parkinson, A.J., Schloss, M.L., Fitzgerald, M.A., Knight, J.A., Murphy, C.M., Kiviat, N.B., Toomey, K.E., Reeves, W.C., Schmid, D.S., & Stamm, W.E. (1994). The prevalence of cervical infection with human papillomaviruses and cervical dysplasia in Alaska Native women. *The Journal of Infectious Diseases, 169,* 792-800.

Dignan, M., Michielutte, R., Blinson, K., Sharp, P., Wells, H.B., & Sands, E. (1993). Cervical cancer prevention: An individualized approach. *Alaska Medicine, 35,* 279-84.

Dignan, M., Michielutte, R., Blinson, K., Wells, H.B., Case, L.D., Sharp, P., Davis, S., Konen, J., & McQuellon, R.P. (1996). Effectiveness of health education to increase screening from cervical cancer among Eastern-Band Cherokee Indian women in North Carolina. *Journal of the National Cancer Institute, 88,* 1670-76.

Han, P.K., Hagel, J., Welty, T.K., Ross, R., Leonardson, G., & Keckler, A. (1994). Cultural factors associated with health-risk behavior among the Cheyenne River Sioux. *American Indian and Alaska Native Mental Health, 5*(3): 15-29.

Healy, B. (1991a). Women's health, public welfare. *Journal of the American Medical Association, 266*, 566-568.

Healy, B. (1991b). The yentl syndrome. *New England Journal of Medicine, 325*, 274-275.

Hunter, D. (1997, June 29). Where it all began. *Anchorage Daily News.*

Hurdle, D., & Tellman, B. (1994). Walk the path to good health for yourself and your family: Learn breast self-examination. [Video] Anchorage, AK: Planned Parenthood of Alaska.

John, M. (1997, September). Cross Cultural Awareness. Paper presented at the annual conference of the Alaska Chapter of the National Association of Social Workers, Anchorage, AK.

Joe, J.R. (1996). The health of American Indian and Alaska Native women. *Journal of the American Medical Women's Association, 51*(4) 141-145.

Kagawa-Singer, M. (1995). Socioeconomic and cultural influences on cancer care of women. *Seminars in Oncology Nursing, 11*(2) 109-119.

Kizzia, T. (1997, June 29). Village or tribes? *Anchorage Daily News.*

Lanier, A.P. (1996). Increase in lung cancer in Alaska Natives: How high will the rates go? *Alaska Medicine, 38*, 38-9.

Lanier, A.P. (1993). Epidemiology of cancer in Alaska Natives. (1993). *Alaska Medicine, 35*, 45-47.

Lanier, A.P., Bulkow, L.R., & Irland, B. (1989). Cancer in Alaskan Indians, Eskimos, and Aleuts 1969-83: Implications for etiology and control. *Public Health Reports, 104*, 658-64.

Lanier, A.P., Kelly, J.J., Smith, B., Amadon, C., Harpster, A., Peters, H., Tanttila, H., Key, C., & Davidson, A.M. (1994). Cancer in the Alaska Native population: Eskimo, Aleut, and Indian incidence and trends 1969-1988. *Alaska Medicine, 36*(1).

Lutz, D.J. (1997). Delivering health care to Native American women: The Challenge Continues. *Obstetrical and Gynecological Survey, 52*(3) 153-54.

Michielutte, R., Sharp, P.C., Dignan, M.B., & Blinson, K. (1994). Cultural issues in the development of cancer control programs for American Indian populations. *Journal of Health Care for the Poor and Underserved, 5*, 280-96.

Miller, B.A., Kolonel, L.N., Bernstein, L., Young, Jr., J.L., Swanson, G.M., West, D., Key, C.R., Liff, J.M., Glover, C.S., Alexander, G.A. (1996). *Racial/Ethnic Patterns of Cancer in the United States 1988-1992*. Bethesda, MD: National Cancer Institute. NIH Pub. No. 96-4104.

Molina, J.W. (1997). Cultural medicine. *Journal for Minority Medical Students*, 28-32.

National Committee on Women's Issues. (1996, March). Proposed policies, by-laws, goals fielded. *NASW News, 41*, 18-19.

Nutting, P.A., Freeman, W.L., Risser, D.R., Helgerson, S.D., Paisano, R., Hisnanick, J., Beaver, S.K., Peters, I., Carney, J.P., & Speers, M.A. (1993). Cancer incidence among American Indians and Alaska Natives, 1980 through 1987. *American Journal of Public Health, 83*, 1589-98.

Olson, M.M. (1994). Introduction: Reclaiming the "other"–Women, health care and social work. *Social Work in Health Care, 19*(3/4), 1-16.

Provost, E.M. (1996). Cervical cancer screening on the Yukon-Kuskokwim Delta, southwest Alaska. *Cancer: Diagnosis, Treatment, Research, 78,* 1598-1602.

Schumacher, C., Landen, M.G., Gessner, B.D., & Beller, M. (1997). Alaska's Healthy People 2000 Health Status Indicators by Region. Anchorage, AK: State of Alaska, Department of Health and Social Services.

Schumacher, C., Lanier, A.P., & Owen, P.G. (1997). *Health risks in Alaska Among Alaska Natives: Behavioral Risk Factor Survey 1991-1993.* Juneau, AK: State of Alaska, Department of Health and Social Services.

Stillwater, B., Echavarria, V.A., & Lanier, A.P. (1995). Pilot test of a cervical cancer prevention video developed for Alaska Native women. *Public Health Reports, 110*(2): 211-14.

Strickland, C.J., Chrisman, N.J., Yallup, M., Powell, K., & Squeoch, M.D. (1996). Walking the journey of womanhood: Yakama Indian women and Papanicolaou (Pap) test screening. *Public Health Nursing, 13,* 141-150.

Harnessing the Positive Power of Language: American Indian Women, a Case Example

Margaret A. Waller
Christina Risley-Curtiss
Sharon Murphy
Anne Medill
Gloria Moore

SUMMARY. Reflecting biases that permeate the U.S. culture, professional accounts generally interpret stories of minority women from a deficit perspective. Problems such as substance abuse, domestic violence, and teenage pregnancy are often presented from an outsider's viewpoint and cast as intrapersonal phenomena independent of historical, political, and cultural context. This article suggests that stories and their implications change significantly depending on

Margaret A. Waller, PhD, is affiliated with the Arizona State University School of Social Work, PO Box 871802, Tempe, AZ 85287.

Christina Risley-Curtiss, MSSW, PhD, is affiliated with the Arizona State University School of Social Work, PO Box 871802, Tempe, AZ 85287.

Sharon Murphy, MSW, ABD, is affiliated with the Arizona State University School of Social Work, PO Box 871802, Tempe, AZ 85287.

Anne Medill, MSW, PhD, is affiliated with Northern Arizona University, Department of Sociology, PO Box 15300, Flagstaff, AZ 86001.

Gloria Moore, MSMFT, is affiliated with the Guiding Star Lodge, 30 West Portland Avenue, Phoenix, AZ 85003.

[Haworth co-indexing entry note]: "Harnessing the Positive Power of Language: American Indian Women, a Case Example." Waller, Margaret A. et al. Co-published simultaneously in *Journal of Poverty* (The Haworth Press, Inc.) Vol. 2, No. 4, 1998, pp. 63-81; and: *Pressing Issues of Inequality and American Indian Communities* (ed: Elizabeth A. Segal and Keith M. Kilty) The Haworth Press, Inc., 1998, pp. 63-81. Single or multiple copies of this article are available for a fee from The Haworth Document Delivery Service [1-800-342-9678, 9:00 a.m. - 5:00 p.m. (EST). E-mail address: getinfo@ haworthpressinc.com].

63

whether they are interpreted from a deficit or strengths perspective. Stories of American Indian Women, in their own voices, are discussed as a case example. *[Article copies available for a fee from The Haworth Document Delivery Service: 1-800-342-9678. E-mail address: getinfo@haworthpressinc.com]*

KEYWORDS. American Indian, Native American, strengths, problem-focused, teenage pregnancy, domestic violence

Wisdom, courage, centeredness, perseverance, determination, greatness, patience, competence, endurance, powerfulness: these words suggest an image of strength, resourcefulness, and resilience. Unfortunately these words are rarely used in professional literature or popular media describing racial or ethnic minority populations. Instead, reflecting biases that permeate U.S. culture, both professional and popular accounts tend to focus on individual, family, and community pathology, abnormality, victimization, and disorder. This article explores the scope, purposes, and consequences of focusing on deficits of minority populations. Through discussion of the narratives of American Indian women of Arizona, the authors provide examples of professional accounts that balance examination of problems with recognition of personal, familial, and cultural resources.

PERSISTENCE OF A DEFICIT FOCUS IN THE HELPING PROFESSIONS

The stories that helping professionals tell about service recipients' lives have a defining effect. This effect can be distinctly positive or negative (White, 1985) because, as Saleebey (1996) cautions, "Words have the power to elevate or destroy" (p. 298), and problem-saturated stories impede the helping process in critical ways. Focusing unilaterally on problems perpetuates inequality and disadvantage by constricting vision and limiting hope in both service recipients and helping professionals.

Although the helping professions are working toward a strengths perspective, there is much to suggest that progress is slow. The social work literature provides an interesting case example, because social work has historically identified itself as a profession that focuses on strengths (Hepworth & Larsen, 1982; Towle, 1945). Saleebey (1992) and other proponents of the strengths perspective (Goldstein, 1990; Hepworth & Larsen, 1982; Schnitzer, 1996; Weick, 1988) have suggested that despite rhetoric to the contrary, social work literature, policies, programs, and direct services continue to maintain a deficit focus. The consequence is that the richly detailed and multifaceted stories service recipients tell are translated into professional language that focuses almost exclusively on problems, weaknesses, failures, pathology, and dysfunction. Schnitzer cites the prevalence of stories that "raise questions about the possible irresponsibility, incompetence, and moral deficiency" of oppressed individuals and groups (Schnitzer, 1996, p. 581). She contends that stories helping professionals tell about poor people both reflect and perpetuate oppressive societal stereotypes. Hence, words chosen by professional helpers have been perpetuating the very conditions of inequality and disadvantage that they were intended to ameliorate.

SOCIAL WORK LITERATURE AND AMERICAN INDIANS

In a review of Social Work Abstracts, the authors identified 171 entries describing articles written about American Indians over the past twenty years (1977-1997). These studies address a broad array of problems within the areas of child welfare, health care, mental health, education, political history, and community. Unfortunately strengths are largely ignored in these accounts. As a result, these stories seem to reduce the identity of American Indians to their problems. The following excerpts from the first line of article abstracts illustrate this deficit focus.

The oppression suffered by Native Americans has so undermined their culture and ability to parent, that child abuse and neglect are frequent problems. (Wilkins, 1993)

The relationship between the federal government and the American Indian is iatrogenic in that it has created a parasitic dependency in the Indian's total life plan which fosters depression. (Horejsi, Craig & Pablo, 1992)

This article analyzes the relevance of contemporary literature in comparative politics to the problem of North American tribal underdevelopment. (Townsley & Goldstein, 1977)

While 21 of the 171 articles mention the need for increased cultural competence, none of the articles focuses on the personal, familial, or cultural resources utilized by American Indians who face adverse life circumstances.

HARNESSING THE POSITIVE POWER OF LANGUAGE

The strengths perspective requires viewing service recipients through a different lens, that is, "in light of their capacities, talents, competencies, possibilities, visions, values, and hopes" (Saleebey, 1996 p. 297). The strengths perspective does not deny the existence of real troubles (Saleebey, 1996) but views individuals, families, and communities in terms of their resources as well as their liabilities. It focuses on what moves people toward health and well-being in spite of adversity (Antonovsky, 1987). It also maintains that a holistic understanding requires recognizing the reality of social and political contexts which victimize individuals and communities by reducing them to their problems. It recognizes that the bureaucracies and organizations of helping, as well as the biases of practitioners, may cloud the lens that makes it possible to see and appreciate the strengths of service recipients.

The concept of empowerment is central to the strengths perspective. Pinderhughes (1995) defines empowerment as "achieving reasonable control over one's destiny, learning to cope constructively with debilitating forces in society, and acquiring the competence to initiate change at the individual and [larger] systems levels" (p. 136). Combining empowerment and strengths perspectives makes it possible to view presenting problems within a more holistic personal and social context. Through this expanded lens, problems that have been viewed as individual and family deficits can be understood as the consequences of efforts to cope with an oppressive social environment (Pinderhughes, 1995). For example, family isolation may be understood as an attempt to cope with a chaotic and unsafe community (Aponte, 1994) or with the broader contexts of poverty and racism (Korin, 1994).

Understanding the connections between unsuccessful coping efforts and the broader social environment paves the way for empowering interventions. For example, isolated families can establish community connections that are nourishing and protective (Auerswald, 1992). Distressed families can establish linkages with natural supports, engage with community groups, and secure needed resources. Education and political action can be used to improve existing structures within the community and create new ones (Pinderhughes, 1995). In these interventions service recipients are empowered as equal partners in the helping process. Thus empowered, service recipients are as much change agents as the practitioners assisting them (Imber-Black, 1990; Saleebey, 1992; Waldegrave, 1990). Such interventions acknowledge the inevitable reciprocal interaction between individual and community resilience (Saleebey, 1997). They all require building nutritive connections between individuals, families, and communities. These connections result in a sense of belonging and create a sense of commitment and caring (Werner & Smith, 1982).

REVISING PROBLEM-SATURATED STORIES: AMERICAN INDIAN WOMEN OF ARIZONA

As suggested by the case example of deficit focused social work abstracts regarding American Indian service recipients, helping professionals must reinterpret existing problem-saturated stories and must learn new ways of interpreting service recipients' stories in ways that reveal potential as well as problems. For instance, the example cited earlier, of the socially isolated family, may be understood as a story of a family's efforts to protect itself from an unsafe community.

The following discussion, using American Indian women in Arizona who are struggling with substance abuse, domestic violence, and teenage pregnancy as a case example, suggests ways that problem-saturated stories about service recipients might be "revisioned" such that strengths as well as problems are apparent. The first step in revisioning these stories is to set them in historical, social, and political context.

Evidence suggests that Indians have populated North and South America for 75,000 years. Tribes spread throughout the Hemisphere, adapting to many physical environments and developing hundreds of cultures, including the complex societies of the Mayans, Incas and Aztecs (Joesphy, 1991).

Contact between American Indian peoples and incoming Europeans has been characterized by conflict and subordination by the European-Americans. Accordingly, American Indians have a long history of having their needs defined by outsiders. The federal government has defined where they would live. Missionaries have defined what they should believe and how they should worship. The Indian Health Service and the Bureau of Indian Affairs have defined their health care and human service needs and have allotted services accordingly.

The first treaty between an American Indian tribe and the U.S. government was signed in 1778. During the next century, over 600 treaties and agreements were made (Lewis, 1995). Ostensibly these treaties constituted negotiations between the federal government and sovereign Indian nations. However, the rights of American Indians were systematically subverted in these agreements and tribes who refused to acquiesce were punished (Schaefer, 1996).

The nineteenth century was devastating for every American Indian tribe. It was during this time that the previously unofficial policy of oppression became official. In 1830, the Indian Removal Act, calling for the relocation of all Eastern Indian tribes across the Mississippi River, was passed. The forced relocation of these tribes continued over a ten-year period and has appropriately been termed "The Trail of Tears" (Schaefer, 1996). In 1871, Congress passed legislation which mandated that no future treaties be entered into with any Indian tribe. This legislation codified the U.S. government's deconstruction of American Indians as citizens of independent nations and reconstructed them as dependents (Lewis, 1995).

Since that time, the primary objective of U.S. policy, including economic, educational, and social welfare policy, has been domination and assimilation of American Indians. Needless to say, these policies have been designed and implemented largely in the absence of input from American Indians themselves (Marger, 1994) who were considered to be culturally inferior and in need of being "Christianized" and "civilized" in order to rise to the level of the dominant society (Lewis, 1995). For example, the Allotment Act of the 1880s (also called the Dawes Act) was designed to weaken tribal institutions and alienate American Indians from their system of common land ownership. Circumventing American Indian structures of leadership and decision making (Lewis, 1995), such as tribal councils and clans, the federal government identified individual males as heads of households and allotted each 160 acres of land (Lewis, 1995, Schaefer, 1996). This practice also subverted the traditional American Indian definition of family in which all members of a clan are considered immediate family. The assumptions behind the Allotment Act were that (1) it was best for American Indians to assimilate into the dominant society, and (2) each individual was best considered apart from his or her tribal identity (Schaefer, 1998, p. 156). Under the pretense of recognizing tribal identity, the Reorganization Act of 1934 was actually another effort to force the assimilation of American Indians into the dominant culture. The Reorganization Act revoked the Allotment Act and allowed tribes to adopt a written constitution and elect a tribal council as well as a council president. However, this system actually subverted traditional structures of tribal government by creating leaders of entire reservations, some of which included several tribes who were antagonistic toward one another. Further, under this system, leaders were elected by majority rule, a concept alien to many tribes. Both of these acts continued the federal practice of imposing majority European-American values and structures on American Indians (Schaefer, 1986).

In 1997, 2,288,000 people in the United States identified themselves as American Indian. Of this group, 808,163 individuals were living on reservations (Bureau of the Census, 1997). While American Indians are usually thrown together into a single category, there are approximately 545 federally recognized tribes in the United States (Bureau of Indian Affairs, 1991). Many of these tribes differ from one another in language, social structure, customs, economics, and religious beliefs (Lujan, 1995).

Women comprise slightly more than half (1,152,000) of the American Indian population and nearly half of them are under the age of 25 years (Bureau of the Census, 1996). Indian women are increasingly moving into the work force (from 48% in 1980 to 55% in 1990). American Indian women, in both rural and urban areas, are employed primarily in administrative support and service jobs. In comparison to other women in the U.S., American Indian women are younger, less educated, have children earlier, and have less income. Additionally, they are more likely to die from motor vehicle accidents, homicide, and alcoholism (Lujan, 1995).

Arizona has the third largest American Indian population in the country (Bureau of Indian Affairs, 1991). In Arizona, there are 26 reservations that occupy approximately 27% of the state's land. The thirteen Arizona tribes include the Paiute, Navajo, Hopi, Havasupai, Hualapai, Yavapai, Apache, Mohave, Chemehuevi, Cocopah, Yaqui, Pima, and the Tohono O'Odham.

The Federal Government has ignored the cultural and historical context of social problems among American Indians and has systematically imposed dominant values in social welfare policy and practice. For example, Duran, Guillory and Tungley (1993) and Allen (1985) suggest that substance abuse, domestic violence, and other crimes among American Indians need to be understood within the context of internalized colonialism and unresolved historical grief (Lujan, 1995).

Federal policy and practice regarding teenage pregnancy and parenting constitute another example of imposition of dominant values on American Indians. For example, among many tribes, pregnancy signifies the continuation of a people whose existence has been continuously threatened by the dominant majority. Hence, within the tribal structure, pregnant females of any age may enjoy acceptance and increased status. These values may also be expressed in negative attitudes toward the use of contraception and the practice of abortion, both of which Indian women may equate with tribal extinction (Echohawk, 1982).

A further manifestation of traditional American Indian values is the view that children are to be treasured and educated, not only by their biological parents and extended families, but also by their entire clan. Accordingly, most children in reservation communities grow up in extended family households under the care of members of multiple generations and are addressed and treated as immediate family by the entire clan (Cross, 1986; Lewis & Ho, 1975; Red-horse, 1980). Current state and federal policies and programs offered to pregnant and parenting teenagers have been designed without regard to these traditional values, and may therefore be irrelevant or ineffective with this population.

MINING FOR STRENGTHS IN STORIES OF ADVERSITY

Paralleling the federal practice of domination and forced assimilation, research into the problems of American Indians is typically conducted by outsiders who classify and attempt to remedy problems without considering the perspectives of the individuals being studied. The biases and limited understanding of the observers may create distortions that highlight deficits, overlook strengths, focus on intrapersonal explanations, and obfuscate the meaning of behavior in cultural context.

Alternatively, understanding stories in personal and ecosystemic context opens new possibilities for identifying strengths and for understanding the cultural context of human experiences. Following are examples of stories of American Indian women who vary in age and come from different geographic locations and diverse lifeways. These narratives come from qualitative doctoral research projects conducted by two of the authors. Sharon Murphy (PhD dissertation in progress) focused on domestic violence experiences of Indian women from various tribes in Arizona, whereas Ann Medill (1997) investigated teenage pregnancy and parenting in the Salt River Pima-Maricopa tribe.

Domestic Violence

The results of several studies have suggested that the personal and the social contexts of adverse life events are inseparable for American Indian women. La Fromboise, Heyle and Ozer (1990), in a study of American Indian college women, found that the young women coped by utilizing social support and interpreting their experiences within a traditional holistic framework in which a sense of order and balance was derived by acknowledging the interconnectedness of family, community, tradition, and universe. In a later study (La Fromboise et al., 1990), the same authors found that American Indian women's coping strategies were also related to age, tribal affiliation, and environment.

In an effort to explore the ways American Indian women interpret and cope with adverse life events, one of the authors conducted a series of interviews with American Indian women who had experienced domestic violence. All of the women interviewed were also coping with addiction, and were currently residing in a substance abuse treatment facility in Arizona. The women represented a variety of tribes, and their stories unfolded in a variety of ways. The stories focused on their experiences of the presence of domestic violence and addiction in their lives and the lives of their children. Viewed from a deficit perspective, these stories depict the ravages of substance abuse, domestic violence, poverty, lack of education and the absence of resources. From a strengths perspective, however, like nesting Russian dolls, each of these stories carries within it a subtext of courage, power, resourcefulness, and resilience, called forth in the effort to survive and grow in the face of adversity.

The Power of Dreams

One source of strength that many of the stories had in common was a significant dream. This dream typically envisioned the restoration of disrupted relationships. For example, Sarai stated:

> I had a dream last night about him. That I was sober and he was sober and our kids were there like nothing happened and he was trying to get back with me . . . my dream was that there had been this year that I had never seen them but yet they still loved me like there was nothing . . . it felt so real, so close . . . I dream of having my family back.

Noel, another participant, noted that she often dreamed of reuniting with her former batterer and returning to the period that predated the drinking and violence, recapturing the relationship that had been an oasis in which she had been able to share her innermost thoughts.

. . . he was a whole different person [when he became abusive], but there would be times when I'd be thinking about him and I'd wish sometimes that it was him instead of the guy I'm with now. I really still loved that guy I first met, that's who I was in love with, not this person that was drinking. I sometimes think like that, I wish you'd never done that.

From a deficit perspective Sarai and Noel might be viewed as victims, whose progress and safety were jeopardized by denial and wishful thinking. From a strengths perspective however, while the possibility of denial and wishful thinking are recognized, these dreams are also appreciated for the possibility that gathering strength from one's dreams may be a coping resource. The ability to dream, to envision renewed relationships, is a strength that solution-focused and cognitive theorists alike can appreciate.

Perseverance

The women interviewed were facing the double jeopardy of a volatile abuser and an unresponsive criminal justice system which exacerbated rather than alleviated their distress. Embedded in their stories are subtexts of gathering the courage to take steps toward self-protection in spite of these barriers. These subtexts reveal the patience and persistence that makes it possible for an American Indian woman to find her way in dark times. These women's stories might be cast as tales of victimhood, yet, examined more closely, each of these stories contains a subtext of courage and resilience.

Jean: It was a way of getting him out of there and being safe while at the same time I hated thinking about him going to jail because I didn't know when he got out of jail how angry he would be or where he would be. At least like I said, if he was at home I knew where he was . . . and I didn't know if I'd walk out the door and he'd be standing there with a knife. Yeah, because when he was in jail I used to call constantly, is he out, is he out, is he out? I mean I used to call every 30 minutes and finally the cop told me "Listen, we'll call you when he's out." Which they didn't.

Some of the stories contained subtexts of women using insight as a coping resource.

> Jean noted: And I think just being able to put everything together, it happened. I'm one of those people that needs to know why before I can fix the problem and I know why now . . . So now if I know why, I think I can fix it. Maybe not fix it, I'll be able to heal, that's what I'll be able to do. I've never been able to do that before. I'm on a real strong road now, I've got a foundation to this thing.

Keeping and Returning to Traditional Ways

A third woman, Helen, related her view that she derived strength from fulfilling her tribe's expectation for women. Accordingly, self-lessness and willingness to fulfill a supportive role were effective coping strategies for her. She described her mother as a model. According to Helen, her mother was always available to support her family. Helen credits her mother with being consistently present for her before, during, and after her struggles with substance abuse and battering. During Helen's lifetime, her mother had maintained a tamale business, participated in cultural traditions, and kept up connections with extended family despite the turbulence around her. From a deficit perspective, Helen's mother might be viewed as an enabler whose own development was constricted by adherence to a narrowly defined gender role. Helen's rendition of the story, however, depicts a woman whose perseverance and adherence to traditional cultural values was a source of self-actualization and inspired her daughter to find the strength to recognize and correct destructive personal behavior patterns. This second interpretation is consistent with the findings of La Fromboise et al. (1990).

Other women's subtexts concern accessing their traditional beliefs and practices as coping resources.

> Betty: I didn't care and that's when I ended up in [the] hospital suicidal and finally I just couldn't take it any more so finally my drinking just went and I finally told myself this is no way to live. And I got back in touch with my traditional [belief] and I started experiencing my spirituality with my traditional

again. And there I found myself again and I found it through my traditional spirituality.

Sarai: I had nothing. I went into a depression. I guess maybe the Creator was always looking out for me, I didn't have nothing, you know, he watched out for me and one day I just snapped out of it and said "Hey, this isn't what I want, I want to get out of this." Not out of the relationship . . . out of the way I was feeling . . . And I started to think in a different way. . . . And I began to feel okay with myself, not okay, but I began to build on it.

Brant describes this sub-story of resourcefulness in the face of oppressive conditions in the following way:

I want to talk about blessings, and endurance, and facing the machine. The everyday shit. The everyday joy. We make no excuses for the way we are, the way we live, the way we paint and write. We are not "stoic" and "noble," we are strong-willed and resisting. (1988, p. 10)

Teenage Pregnancy and Parenting

Another of the authors gathered stories of teenage pregnancy and parenting from a group of Pima-Maricopa teenage mothers, all of whom lived on the Salt River Pima-Maricopa reservation just north of Phoenix, Arizona. The reservation is located on approximately 55,000 acres of land and is surrounded by affluent non-Indian communities. According to the Tribal Enrollment Office, in 1995 there were 5,600 enrolled tribal members, 50% of whom were under the age of 18. The community has distinct geographic, cultural, and social boundaries. For example, members who leave the reservation often return because of the difficulty of surviving economically without the support of the tribe. Individuals continue the tradition of identifying all tribal members as kin. A number of homes are without running water, indoor toilets, or heating and air conditioning systems. Many families rely on wood burning stoves on subfreezing winter nights and sleep outdoors during the summer to gain relief from the heat which can exceed 100 degrees for extended periods between the months of May and September.

Positive Cultural Identity

For the young women interviewed, stories of poverty and early pregnancy contain subtexts of strength derived from a positive cultural identity and a sense of being supported by their families and community. The young women's sense of positive cultural identity is indicated in the following excerpts:

Martha: I don't know, I think it's better, the way I was raised . . . with different beliefs, I guess.

Alice: The [Pima] culture is alive for everybody if they want it to be. I don't know, I think this generation is kind of dying because half the kids my age don't know their ancestors or language, or don't know where they came from, their ancestors or anything. But I want my baby to adopt the culture, and like we'll both learn about it together.

Ninebah: I don't think I'd rather be any other race. I love this culture and it's something spiritual. I would like to see more cultural things in the community.

Christine: You know, [being American Indian gives me] a sense of being different, just a little different from the next person. I can tell them, you know, I'm Indian and I'm proud of it. I want to raise my children in a traditional way. I want them to know about who they are and where they come from.

Family Interdependence

The resource of family support was evident in the expectation and acceptance of interdependence within the extended families of the young women interviewed. Their stories depicted them assisting in the caretaking responsibilities for younger relatives and sharing resources such as housing, transportation, and money with parents, siblings, and extended family members.

Kris, a 17-year-old mother, lives with her grandmother:

My mom gives her some of my social security money so that me and the baby can stay with her. It's alright.

Alice, a 16-year-old teen mother, remembers always taking care of her sister because her mother was unavailable:

> Me and my other sister are raising the little ones. I felt like I had to parent.

Community Acceptance

The stories told by these young women also suggested that early pregnancy does not have the negative connotation among the Pima-Maricopa that it does in the majority American society.

> Marla: I don't see the community trying to stop it (teen pregnancy). I know they talk about it a lot, you know, but I don't see them doing anything.

> Esther: I think it's tolerated. Yeah, everybody's just like, Oh, and they don't tell them, you know, not to have babies.

> Pricilla: . . . to me it's just something that happened. There's some kids at 15 besides me that got pregnant. The community, they talk about it, but now it's like more and more the talk's just fading away.

For these teenage mothers, pregnancy does not seem to be perceived as the object of social stigma or as an adverse life event that sets off a series of negative consequences. Instead, these stories suggest that for the Pima-Maricopa a different paradigm may exist which views early pregnancy as an expectable life event rather than as a social problem to be eradicated. This perspective characterizes other American Indian tribes as well. For example, Paula Gunn Allen (1997) provides this window into the teachings of her Laguna Pueblo elders.

> No child is ever considered illegitimate among the Indians, they [the elders] said. If a girl gets pregnant, the baby is still part of the family, and the mother is too. That's what they said, and they showed me real people who lived according to these principles.

Of course the ravages of colonization have taken their toll; there are orphans in Indian country now . . . there are even illegitimate children, though the very concept still strikes me as absurd . . . [however] through all the centuries of war and death and cultural and psychic destruction have endured the women who raise the children and tend the fires, who pass along the tales and the traditions, who weep and bury the dead, who are the dead, and who never forget. There are always the women, who make pots and weave baskets, who fashion clothes and cheer their children on at powwow, who make fry bread and piki bread, and corn soup and chili stew, who dance and sing and remember and hold within their hearts the dream of their ancient peoples–that one day the Woman Who Thinks will speak to us again, and everywhere there will be peace.

CONCLUSION

The social work literature regarding American Indians is an example of the extent to which professional stories about racial and ethnic minority groups can be deficit focused. This deficit focus may result in social welfare policies and practices that perpetuate rather than remedy social problems in a variety of ways. Focusing on problems of minority groups without also highlighting strengths may reinforce an exploitative power relationship in which service recipients' rich and complex stories are drowned out by problem-saturated professional stories. These pathology-focused versions cast service recipients as incompetent, powerless, and passive victims of negative life circumstances which set them on an inevitable downhill course. Such narratives may overlook the social, cultural, political, and historical contexts of human behavior and may fail to reflect the reciprocal interaction between individual behavior and these larger systemic contexts. For example, current social welfare policy does not take into account the meanings attached to early pregnancy in the Pima-Maricopa community. Consequently, policies that reflect dominant societal beliefs may be ineffective and may reinforce the marginalized status of Pima-Maricopa women. Perhaps the most costly consequence of pathology-focused accounts is interventions that fail to access and utilize individual, family, and cultural resources.

Alternatively, professional helpers who seek to adopt a strengths perspective have a rich resource in service recipients' stories. Integrating professional observations with personal narratives broadens the field of observation. Personal stories can be mined for personal, familial, and cultural resources upon which service recipients might draw in times of stress. The stories told by the women in this paper are subtexts within the dominant narratives of substance abuse, domestic violence, and adolescent pregnancy. These subtexts highlight strengths that might be overlooked by problem-focused professional accounts. For example, the stories of Martha and Alice show how they derived strength from a strong sense of cultural identity. Betty's story reflects the healing power of renewed interest and participation in traditional cultural beliefs and practices. The accounts of Sarai and Noel show how they were empowered and comforted by their dreams and visions. Helen describes being heartened by her family legacy of fortitude and perseverance in the face of hard times. Jean's is a story of persistence in spite of an unresponsive criminal justice system. Kris and Alice describe ways their experience of familial and community acceptance and support have fortified them.

Considered in historical, sociopolitical, and cultural context, service recipients' stories contain valuable information. These subtexts within the dominant culture's plots can provide both professional helpers and service recipients with a salutogenic view that deficit-focused professional stories cannot provide.

In the effort to adopt a strengths perspective, and to facilitate more culturally competent services, social welfare researchers, policymakers, and practitioners will find a gold mine in service recipients' stories.

REFERENCES

Allen, P.G. (1985). Violence and the American Indian woman. In *Working together to prevent sexual and domestic violence*, 5(4). Seattle, WA: Center for the Prevention of Sexual and Domestic Violence.

Allen, P.G. (1997). Where I come from is like this. In L. Richardson, V. Taylor, & N. Whittier, Eds. *Feminist Frontiers IV.* New York: McGraw-Hill.

Antonovsky, A. (1987). *Unravelling the mystery of health.* San Francisco: Jossey-Bass.

Aponte, H. (1994). *Bread and spirit: Therapy with the new poor.* New York: W.W. Norton.

Auerswald, E. (1992). The roots of dissonance in human affairs: Epistemological hostagehood and escape therefrom. In J. Mason, J. Rubenstein, & S. Shuda (Eds.), *From diversity to healing: Papers from the 5th biennial international conference of the South African Institute of Marital and family Therapy.* South Africa: Department of Social Work, University of Durban-Westville.

Brant, B. (1988). *A gathering of spirit.* Ithaca, NY: Firebrand Books.

Bureau of the Census. (1996). *Statistical abstract of the United States.* Washington, DC: US Government Printing Office.

Bureau of Indian Affairs. (1991). *American Indians today:Answers to your questions (3rd ed.).* Washington, DC: United States Department of the Interior.

Cross, T.L. (1986). Drawing on cultural tradition in Indian child welfare. *Social Casework, 67,* 283-289.

Duran, E., Guillory, B., & Tingley, P. (1993). Domestic violence in Native American communities: The effects of intergenerational post traumatic stress. Unpublished manuscript.

Echohawk, M. (1982). Sexual consequences of acculturation of American Indian women. In M. Kirkpatrick (Ed.) *Women's sexual experience.* NY: Plenum Press.

Goldstein, H. (1990). Strength or pathology: Ethical and rhetorical contrasts in approaches to practice. *Families in Society, 71,* 267-275.

Hepworth, D. & Larsen, J. (1982). *Direct social work practice.* Homewood, IL: Dorsey Press.

Horejsi, C., Craig, B.H.R., & Pablo, J. (1992). Reactions by Native American parents to child protection agencies: Cultural and community factors. *Child Welfare, 29,* 329-342.

Imber-Black, E. (1990). Multiple embedded systems. In M. Mirkin (Ed.), *The social and political contexts of family therapy* (pp. 3-18). New York: Allyn and Bacon.

Joesphy, A. (1991). *The Indian heritage of America.* New York: Houghton Mifflin.

Korin, E. (1994). Social inequalities and therapeutic relationships: Applying Freire's ideas to clinical practice. In R. Almeida (Ed.), *Expansions of feminist family therapy through diversity* (pp. 75-98). New York: The Haworth Press, Inc.

La Fromboise, T., Heyle, A., & Ozer, E. (1990). Changing and diverse roles of women in American Indian cultures. *Sex Roles, 22,* 455-473.

Lewis, R. G., & Ho, M.K. (1975). Social work with Native Americans. *Social Work, 20,* 379-382.

Lewis, R.G. (1995). American Indians. In R.L. Edwards et al. (Eds.) *Encyclopedia of Social Work* (19th ed. pp. 216-225). Washington, DC: National Association of Social Workers.

Lujan, C.C. (1995). Women warriors: American Indian women, crime and alcohol. *Women and Criminal Justice, 7*, 9-33.

Marger, M.N. (1994). *Race and ethnic relations: American and global perspectives.* 3rd ed. Belmont, CA: Wadsworth.

Murphy, S. (in progress) American Indian women's lived experience of domestic violence: A phenomenological approach. Unpublished doctoral dissertation, Arizona State University, Tempe, AZ.

Medill, A. (1997). Unpublished doctoral dissertation, University of Michigan.

Pinderhuges, E. (1995). Empowering diverse populations: Family practice in the 21st century. *Families in Society, 76*,131-140.

Redhorse, J.G. (1980). American Indian elders: Unifiers of Indian families. *Social Casework, 61*, 490-493.

Saleebey, D. (1997). Community development, group empowerment, and individual resilience. In D. Saleebey (Ed.), *The strengths perspective in social work practice.* (2nd ed., 200-215).

Saleebey, D. (1992). *The strengths perspective in social work practice.* New York: Longman.

Saleebey, D. (1996). The strengths perspective in social work practice: Extensions and cautions. *Social Work, 41*, 296-305.

Schaefer, R.T. (1998). *Racial and ethnic groups.* 7th ed. New York: Longman.

Schnitzer, P. (1996). "The don't come in!" Stories told, lessons taught about poor families in therapy. *American Journal of Orthopsychiatry, 66(4)* pp. 572-582.

Towle, C. (1945). A social work approach to courses in growth and behavior. *Social Service Review, 34*, 402-414.

Townsley, H.C., & Goldstein, G.S. (1977). One view of the etiology of depression in the American Indian. *Public Health Reports, 15*, 458-461.

Waldegrave, C. (1990). Just therapy. *Dulwich Centre Newsletter, 1*, 5-46.

Weick, A., Rapp, C., Sullivan, W.P., & Kisthardt, S. (1989). A strengths perspective for social work practice. *Social Work, 34*, 350-354.

Werner, E. & Smith, R.S. (1982). *Vulnerable but invincible.* New York: McGraw-Hill.

White, M. (1985). Fear busting and monster taming: An approach to the fears of young children. *Dulwich Centre Review.* Adelaide, South Australia: Dulwich Centre.

Wilkins, D.E. (1993). Modernization, colonialism, dependency: How appropriate are these models for providing an explanation of North American Indian "underdevelopment?" *Ethnic and Racial Studies, 30*, 390-419.

THOUGHTS ON POVERTY AND INEQUALITY

Injustice Experienced

Editor's Note: The following is excerpted from the writings of an American Indian woman who wished to remain anonymous. I thank her for her willingness to share her experience. The everyday inequality experienced by members of non-dominant groups is often lost on the dominant culture or it is claimed that such acts do not occur, that everyone is treated equally. Unfortunately this is not true, and this incident reminds us of that reality.

When I review all the places I've lived, I can't remember vividly any places that I felt discriminated against. Maybe it was just ignorance or maybe I never paid attention like I do now. I hate to say it, but Arizona is the place that I experience the most prejudice and stereotyping. For me, it's just a way of life, but I'm very proud of who I am. I am at peace with myself. We don't choose what color our skin is or who our neighbors might be. We all are here for some purpose. Everyone knows history. It doesn't really matter who was first, second, or third in getting here. It is still one world. Everyone

[Haworth co-indexing entry note]: "Injustice Experienced." Anonymous. Co-published simultaneously in *Journal of Poverty* (The Haworth Press, Inc.) Vol. 2, No. 4, 1998, pp. 83-84; and: *Pressing Issues of Inequality and American Indian Communities* (ed: Elizabeth A. Segal and Keith M. Kilty) The Haworth Press, Inc., 1998, pp. 83-84. Single or multiple copies of this article are available for a fee from The Haworth Document Delivery Service [1-800-342-9678, 9:00 a.m. - 5:00 p.m. (EST). E-mail address: getinfo@haworthpressinc.com].

83

destroys it. Everyone suffers or everyone benefits. Everyone's purpose depends on your perspective.

OCTOBER 2, 1997

I'm cruising main street in a red Trans Am. I see a truck in a used car lot. I go to the next block to turn around, I want to check it out. The next thing I know a cop is on my tail. Another cop shooting radar motions me to pull in front of ten cars. Now, common sense would say that if I'm speeding, why would I drive directly back to where the officer was shooting radar? An officer comes to my window and proceeds to yell at me, "What in the hell are you going 53 in a 35." I look at him dumbfounded. His partner assumes I'm extremely dangerous. He pulls a revolver, aims it at my head. I realize, I'm in serious trouble. I proceed to ask, "Why does your buddy have a pistol at my head." He tells me not to get smart. He motions to his buddy to put the revolver up. He asks, "Is this your car?" I said, "Yes." He tells me not to get smart.

OCTOBER 31, 1997

I go to court. I'm not on the docket. They say come back on November 25, 1997. I'm worried and still wondering what made that officer act so aggressively. Wondering, if I had flinched or made a rapid arm movement, what would have been the result?

NOVEMBER 25, 1997

I go to court. The whole incident is dismissed. I still wonder what could have happened. At court, I asked the officer about his trigger happy buddy. His response, "You should be glad he didn't get a radar caliber reading." Huh! What would have happened if I was someone else?

Ascending Poverty and Inequality in Native America: An Alternative Perspective

Shaunna McCovey

When people attempt to define poverty it is most often looked at in regards to the Gross National Product (GNP), an interpretation of material exchanges. If one has accumulated a significant amount of material goods, then one is considered wealthy. Any deficiency in such goods, and one would be viewed as poor.

I would like to look at poverty and inequality in another way, offer a less restricted view, and go so far as to define poverty as culture; to see it not in terms of dollars and cents, but rather a phenomenon that has allowed tradition, heritage, and values to flourish among Indian peoples.

My Yurok people have occupied the mountainous regions surrounding the Klamath River in Northern California for centuries. We have survived invasion, disease, and the wrath of white greed and murder that accompanied the gold rush. No word better describes Yuroks and other Native Americans than "resilient," and the same story can be told from reservation to reservation.

I could continue to discuss the misfortunes of the American Indian, how nearly one-third of us live in poverty as defined by the GNP, how the government has mistreated us for hundreds of years, and how Manifest Destiny most certainly became our destiny, but I

Shaunna McCovey (*Yurok/Karuk*) is affiliated with Arizona State University.

[Haworth co-indexing entry note]: "Ascending Poverty and Inequality in Native America: An Alternative Perspective." McCovey, Shaunna. Co-published simultaneously in *Journal of Poverty* (The Haworth Press, Inc.) Vol. 2, No. 4, 1998, pp. 85-87; and: *Pressing Issues of Inequality and American Indian Communities* (ed: Elizabeth A. Segal and Keith M. Kilty) The Haworth Press, Inc., 1998, pp. 85-87. Single or multiple copies of this article are available for a fee from The Haworth Document Delivery Service [1-800-342-9678, 9:00 a.m. - 5:00 p.m. (EST). E-mail address: getinfo@haworthpressinc.com].

won't. I would rather not sing the tune to the same old song. It has been played out.

Instead I would like to offer an alternative point of view and look at poverty and inequality as necessary for us to continue as Indian peoples. And I would begin with this bold statement: We haven't forgotten how to survive.

We are not just dealing with poverty and inequality as definitions any longer, it's now about our survival as people, Tribes and Nations. Our survival depends upon our ability to ascend to a new spiritual awareness or, perhaps, find an old one, and fight for our existence on that level. We cannot fight physically, because we are out-numbered. We cannot fight economically, because we hold no monetary wealth. We cannot fight psychologically, because we do not have volumes of written text to back up or justify our actions. We can, however, fight spiritually because when we believe that our dances help fix the Earth; they do. And when we believe that we are dancing and praying not only for ourselves, but for everything that lives and breathes; we are.

We live in a society that does nothing to accommodate us, therefore we must make our own accommodations. If we continue to dwell on our so-called misfortunes, how do we expect to move beyond their grasp? If we cannot begin to see ourselves in a less oppressed condition, how will we ever overcome that oppression?

Poverty and inequality have enabled us to continue our way of life. Had we been granted lives of upper- or middle-class luxury would we have continued to be as strong culturally as we are today? Probably not. We remember what the importance of survival is. Something that luxury quickly takes away the moment it steps foot in our homes.

But we also must look at poverty and inequality as obstructions in the path of our survival. We have to acknowledge them for what they have contributed without giving them too much power. If we let them control us we are no longer a people who think consciously about our role on this planet. We become lost in unawareness, absorbed in trying to find a way around the obstructions–looking for answers that we won't find unless we return to our traditions, our spirituality, and view the world and our situation from a higher place.

We are impoverished only if we allow ourselves to be. We are treated unequally only if we perceive it to be true. What many of us do not realize is that we possess an innate ability to see beyond the corners poverty and inequality have created for us as Indian peoples. We need to trust that ability along with the importance and responsibility of validating these truths that we carry within ourselves. The notion has not left us, we need only to summon it once again.

While we may be perceived as poor by those who gave us the definition, we will never be poor in spirit. While we may be dominated by inequality, we will never allow it to break us. We cannot escape our economic disparity, but we can turn it into a spiritual awareness, a culmination of where we have been, who we are, and where we are going.

As we move deeper into the technological age, and survival becomes a much easier task, we cannot doubt the ability that we have developed to adapt, to live in both worlds without forgetting what it means to be Indian, no matter which Tribe we represent. If we let technology and all that accompanies it take away from our cultural, traditional, and spiritual beliefs, then we become lumped in the same category as those who do not remember how to survive, those who search for meaning in that which meaning does not exist.

Whether I'm right or wrong about that which I speak is yet to be determined. I feel that if we do not think about these things and, perhaps, turn thought into action, we will remain stagnant, and when something remains stagnant for a lengthy period of time it begins to die. And we are survivors.

Being labeled poor has allowed us to remember how to dance and sing in a traditional way, and for this we are rich. Being thought of as unequal has forced us to rely on our knowledge of culture to survive, and this knowledge is wealth.

We have to remember that poverty and inequality are simply a state of mind and a spiritual ascension of the two may guarantee our survival well into the next thousand years.

Weaving My Way:
The Cultural Construction
of Writing in Higher Education

Alicia Fedelina Chávez

Recently, during a faculty departmental retreat, I felt compelled to share my frustrating experience of trying to write a dissertation within the confines of a university process that felt incredibly unnatural to me. A year into my new faculty position, far away from my doctoral institution and long after my advisor and I assured my colleagues I would be finished, I felt an obligation to express my ongoing fears, frustrations and recent revelations concerning my writing. I had been feeling an increasing sense of panic at my slow progress with this dissertation on which my job depended.

During a departmental faculty retreat session in which we shared our research, I painfully described my struggles and shared a recent discovery that the process I use to write does not seem to be a normative one in higher education environments. I shared that I had been unable to write for the past year under the strict linear guidelines set down by my dissertation advisor. Her expectation was that I send her one chapter at a time and wait for approval before going on to the next step. During this session, I haltingly tried to describe the process that I have always used to write. At the end of my story,

Alicia Fedelina Chávez is affiliated with the Department of Educational Leadership, Miami University, 350 McGuffey Hall, Oxford, OH 45056 (e-mail: chavezaf@ muohio.edu).

[Haworth co-indexing entry note]: "Weaving My Way: The Cultural Construction of Writing in Higher Education." Chávez, Alicia Fedelina. Co-published simultaneously in *Journal of Poverty* (The Haworth Press, Inc.) Vol. 2, No. 4, 1998, pp. 89-93; and: *Pressing Issues of Inequality and American Indian Communities* (ed: Elizabeth A. Segal and Keith M. Kilty) The Haworth Press, Inc., 1998, pp. 89-93. Single or multiple copies of this article are available for a fee from The Haworth Document Delivery Service [1-800-342-9678, 9:00 a.m. - 5:00 p.m. (EST). E-mail address: getinfo@haworthpressinc.com].

© 1998 by The Haworth Press, Inc. All rights reserved.

as I sat shaking from the effort, a new faculty colleague, recently hired and also Native American, walked quietly over to me and whispered, "Alicia, you just described *my* writing process."

How was it that at the age of 35, now a college professor, I have suddenly been jolted into a realization that I write differently and that it may be culturally based in the ways that I conceptualize? How is it that without realizing it, I developed a way to write successfully for so many years despite mainstream educational systems? Could it be that I have worked so hard to become an educator and challenge mainstream systems only to be turned back at the final gate?

I am currently a full-time tenure-track faculty member who was hired "ABD" (all but dissertation) into a department of Educational Leadership. My leadership, activism, teaching, research and writing revolve around the question of how institutions of higher education need to change to effectively educate a diversity of students for an increasingly pluralistic society. For the first time in my life, I am struggling against an educational barrier that I just can't seem to go over or around. Throughout my education, I have gone over, under, around or through cultural barriers of language, misinterpretation, harassment, exclusion and invisibility. Now I am experiencing a sustained difficulty with my dissertation because of a seemingly reasonable process required by my dissertation advisor and common to many doctoral programs. Though there are a variety of ways to complete any task, I am being required to utilize a culturally constructed process endorsed by my advisor. Because she is unable or perhaps unwilling to consider a different process of writing, I am struggling painfully and unsuccessfully.

Throughout the spring and summer of last year, I worked hard but was unable to produce chapters in the linear, chronological order required by my dissertation advisor. Finally, out of desperation, I informed her that I needed to utilize my own non-linear process and send her the whole draft rather than one chapter at a time. I tried to explain that, though I would still process continually with her, I was unable to work within her expected linear process. Although I couldn't find the words at the time to explain why, I did not feel that any of the chapters could form without the whole. I did know, somehow, that this "knowing" went deeper than the common dilemma faced by doctoral students that their work could always be a little bit better.

I conceptualize my writing metaphorically, as the creation of multi-dimensional tapestries. I am the weaver through which a tapestry forms. Writing is more complex than just the product created; it is a relationship between the writer and the written. As I review literature and collect data I begin to see strands of thought that slowly interweave to form patterns. Some of these patterns weave through the entire tapestry and others collect to form smaller patterns within. All eventually connect in complex ways throughout. Much of this process is without written word as I watch patterns emerge and reemerge in the data, the literature, my experiences and my connection to the work. Eventually I begin to write as the patterns become more distinct in my inner vision. A linear, chapter-focused process, like that required by my dissertation advisor, places my work under an assumption that one step can and should be completed before something else is understood. It is based also on an assumption that we can understand the whole only by looking at each part individually in a step-by-step process. This does not work for me. I was taught that in order to understand we must be able to see the many strands, the patterns *and* the whole; that each informs the other and that most importantly, the weaver influences what is seen and how it forms. There is then, a relationship between the weaver and the tapestry. We glimpse the tapestry through the weaver and the weaver through the tapestry.

As a highly intuitive "Mestiza" (Native American and Latina) individual raised in the northern mountains of New Mexico, I trust and rely on my intuitive voice. I was raised to believe that it is critical for me to listen to more than just the voices of my 5 senses. Just before that fall faculty retreat, I felt a strong intuitive pull to read a book by a favorite author, Gloria Anzaldua entitled *Borderlands/La Frontera: The New Mestiza*. This work is about those of us who come from a mix of Latin and Native American cultures, intermingling since the 1500s in the Americas and no longer distinguishable as two cultures. Her use of a written rhythm that I could *feel*, triggered an incredible revelation for me about my writing. I began to realize the impact of my non-linear way of writing and conceptualizing on my dissertation process. For the first time in my life, as a part of a standardized process, I was being required to utilize a linear process to write . . . and it was unnatural and immobilizing for me. Asking for and approving dissertation chapters one after the other is a highly standardized expectation in many doctoral programs and its linear assumption is something that is profoundly silencing to my writing process.

Through repeated failed attempts at this process and through reflection, I came to understand that I have successfully negotiated formal public education by first utilizing my own natural non-linear writing process and then reformatting it to "fit into" standard linear writing structures. . . . "say what you are going to say . . . say it. . . . say what you said." Until now, I have been able to use my own multi-step process because teachers always asked only for the finished product rather than for sections or chapters. This enabled me to utilize my own process but also kept me from learning that my process might be different. I assumed that everyone must use a multi-step process to write. Even my master's thesis advisor utilized this process with me. We met regularly to discuss my work but for whatever reason, he asked only to read the final draft. This enabled me once again to utilize a non-linear process and then reformat it to fit the required structure.

So you may ask, why stay with this advisor who insists on the use of a linear process? You may assume that it would be difficult to find an advisor who knows about, understands and values non-linear writing processes. You would be right. I have never talked with anyone in higher education who opened the door to the possibility of non-linear conceptualizing or writing . . . not until I read *Borderlands/La Frontera*. But there is another, more culturally compelling reason that I have stayed with my advisor. I was taught that relationships are long term and to expect and value the work of maintaining and improving them. Loyalty in relationships is a critical part of both Native American and Latin cultures and I valued and was loyal to my advisor. Further, the teacher-student relationship is a "sacred" relationship that holds a special place in both cultures. I was taught that many times the student will not understand the reasons behind what a teacher does. The student is taught to put their trust in the teacher and in return, the teacher must hold that trust sacred. When cultures mix, however, as in this relationship, there can be no assumption of the definition of the relationship and difficulties are likely to arise.

Though I try, I do not have the words or even a very clear understanding to explain and negotiate the dissertation process with my advisor. She perhaps does not have the ability or willingness to understand. As I write this, I am waiting to hear from her after sending my dissertation in almost full draft form. Her last chilling words ring in my mind, *"I am used to approving one chapter at a time. Expect major revisions."*

I am slowly weaving words and ideas together to form a tapestry that is my dissertation. Strands of thought interweave and patterns reveal themselves to me as I work. Yet the incredible creative process of writing for me continues to be stifled by someone who, perhaps with good intention, values and guards the culturally constructed gates of academe. Am I as Mestiza, as emerging voice, as culturally other, to be locked out?

Index

Haworth
DOCUMENT DELIVERY
SERVICE

This valuable service provides a single-article order form for any article from a Haworth journal.

- *Time Saving:* No running around from library to library to find a specific article.
- *Cost Effective:* All costs are kept down to a minimum.
- *Fast Delivery:* Choose from several options, including same-day FAX.
- *No Copyright Hassles:* You will be supplied by the original publisher.
- *Easy Payment:* Choose from several easy payment methods.

Open Accounts Welcome for . . .
- Library Interlibrary Loan Departments
- Library Network/Consortia Wishing to Provide Single-Article Services
- Indexing/Abstracting Services with Single Article Provision Services
- Document Provision Brokers and Freelance Information Service Providers

---

MAIL or *FAX* THIS ENTIRE ORDER FORM TO:

Haworth Document Delivery Service
The Haworth Press, Inc.
10 Alice Street
Binghamton, NY 13904-1580

or FAX: 1-800-895-0582
or CALL: 1-800-429-6784
9am-5pm EST

PLEASE SEND ME PHOTOCOPIES OF THE FOLLOWING SINGLE ARTICLES:
1) Journal Title: _____
     Vol/Issue/Year: _____Starting & Ending Pages:_____
Article Title:_____
_____

2) Journal Title: _____
     Vol/Issue/Year: _____Starting & Ending Pages:_____
Article Title:_____
_____

3) Journal Title: _____
     Vol/Issue/Year: _____Starting & Ending Pages:_____
Article Title:_____
_____

4) Journal Title: _____
     Vol/Issue/Year: _____Starting & Ending Pages:_____
Article Title:_____
_____

(See other side for Costs and Payment Information)

COSTS: Please figure your cost to order quality copies of an article.

1. Set-up charge per article: $8.00
   ($8.00 × number of separate articles) _____
2. Photocopying charge for each article:
   1-10 pages: $1.00 _____

   11-19 pages: $3.00 _____

   20-29 pages: $5.00 _____

   30+ pages: $2.00/10 pages _____

3. Flexicover (optional): $2.00/article _____
4. Postage & Handling: US: $1.00 for the first article/
   $.50 each additional article _____

   Federal Express: $25.00 _____

   Outside US: $2.00 for first article/
   $.50 each additional article _____

5. Same-day FAX service: $.50 per page _____

   GRAND TOTAL: _____

METHOD OF PAYMENT: (please check one)
❏ Check enclosed   ❏ Please ship and bill. PO # _____
(sorry we can ship and bill to bookstores only! All others must pre-pay)
❏ Charge to my credit card: ❏ Visa; ❏ MasterCard; ❏ Discover;
                            ❏ American Express;

Account Number: _____ Expiration date: _____

Signature: **✗** _____

Name: _____ Institution: _____

Address: _____

_____

City: _____ State: _____ Zip: _____

Phone Number: _____ FAX Number: _____

MAIL or *FAX* THIS ENTIRE ORDER FORM TO:

Haworth Document Delivery Service	**or FAX:** 1-800-895-0582
The Haworth Press, Inc.	**or CALL:** 1-800-429-6784
10 Alice Street	(9am-5pm EST)
Binghamton, NY 13904-1580	